INFLATION?   TRY A BICYCLE.

BY

P.J. EMERSON

£3.00

First published 1978
Printed in Northern Ireland
by The Northern Whig Limited
Belfast

ISBN 0 9506028 0 9

They called him Baha.

To those boys, who are men, who were men, this book is dedicated, for Baha believes that if they do not succumb to the materialism or corruption of some of their European and African superiors (an oft used misnoma), Kenya will be a great country.

PREFACE

If, when you meet and start chatting with Baha, he suddenly leans back, crosses his fingers over his ever expanding waist, pats this bulging gut with his thumbs, casts his eyes to the nether-world and starts, slowly,

"Ah yes....I remember....when I was in...." then you should tell him to shut up.

ACKNOWLEDGEMENTS

My sincere thanks are due to two:

to Dervla Murphy, who wrote the foreword, for her wonderful encouragements and great humour. Her companionship I enjoy, but with slight reservation if and when we go cycling together. I can and do roll along, fast or slow, in somewhat amateurish fashion, but I feel when in her company, that I'm with the maestro.

and to Judy Howard, who has at least two major talents. Firstly, she can draw magnificently, and hers are the pictures in this book. And secondly, her politeness knows no bounds, for she repeatedly praised my childish doodles.

And my sincere no thanks are due to bank managers and various officials of odd government agencies who seem to have no idea of how difficult it might be to return form rhubarb rhubarb in triplicate when one is on a bicycle in the bush of Africa.

ACKNOWLEDGEMENTS

CONTENTS

FOREWORD

People who spend most of their waking hours writing books, reviewing books or helping publishers to decide whether or not typescripts should become books — such people look upon yet another typescript with cold detachment. It has to have something extra to arouse enthusiasm. And INFLATION? has something extra. As I am not trying to review it I don't have to say what; I can leave it to each reader to find out for himself. An interesting point about this book is that different readers may well come to a different conclusions about *why* they have enjoyed it. It exists on more than one level, as all good writing must, and it stimulates in an exciting yet relaxing way, like the best sort of conversation.

In this post-lunar age, it is quite difficult to engage people's attention with a travel book about merely terrestrial journeys. Fifty years ago it was enough to have gone on a tiger-shoot in Mysore State with ten elephants, twenty mahouts, seventy coolies, five personal servants and the Maharaja's third cousin. After that you could write a thickish tome in painful English — MY DAYS WITH GUN AND TENT AS A ROYAL GUEST — and be sure of steady sales. It is pleasing to reflect that in the intervening years certain standards have gone *up*. Now even walking across the Antarctic on your hands is not enough unless the subsequent story is told with some originality of thought and distinction of style.

Peter Emerson brings both these qualities to INFLATION? There is nothing commonplace in these pages and there is an amount of wisdom here, of the sort that springs not from age and experience but from an inborn flair for getting priorities right. There is also a great deal of humanity, which is the most important traveller's virtue; and it is especially important when, as in the present case, it is based not only on an ethical code but on an imaginative capacity to demolish all the conventional barriers between races. And there is a sensitivity that never becomes mawkish, and a humour that often depends deliciously on an unexpected dart of the mind, and a gift for exact, concise descriptions that seem very matter-of-fact yet have the rare power of making us feel familiar with the unfamiliar. Some of us who have worked hard for years at the craft of writing will never attain the natural literary skill displayed in these pages.

There are of course flaws here and Peter Emerson's next book will be even better; in any artist's world, there is always room for improvement. If this were not so, people would stop creating, since the artistic act of creation is powered by a longing for unattainable perfection. But none of these flaws detracts from the enjoyment of a remarkable book by a remarkable young writer.

DERVLA MURPHY

ix

LIST OF MAPS — GUIDE TO COUNTRIES

---

*a rough translation might read: The Rt. Hon. Sir Charles Augustus Thaythornthwaite-Smythe Junior, Baronet, ABC, DE, F.

KEY TO MAPS

——————————— national borders

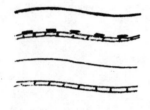 national borders which should be midstream

——————————— big rivers*

enormous rivers

– – – – – – – big rivers in rainy seasons, but for most of the year, they are but empty river beds*.

*some rivers, a close inspection of the maps will reveal, don't go anywhere. Most rivers (blue) go eventually to the sea (blue), but these just disappear into the blue (white), ending in swamps and/or evaporation.

  lakes

  seasonal lakes

possible flood areas, adjoining Lake Chad

  swamps

  game parks

 escarpments, either side of the rift valley

xii

∧ ∧ ∧
∧ ∧ ∧ ∧
∧ ∧ ∧ ∧   mountains
∧ ∧ ∧
∧

⋀   volcanoes

▵ 5119 m
16743 ft   mountains of altitude as shown

● NAIROBI 1661 m
5450 ft   towns and cities

Baha's route:

when on his bicycle

in a dug-out canoe

on a river boat

in a train

in a lorry, the bike having broken down

or firmly under arrest.

xiii

INTRODUCTION

If someone has written a book about a journey, one may assume it was successful if not enjoyable. Few spend months and pounds only to say how terrible everything was, and few like to answer negatively to enquiries of adventure, excitement or danger.

Often, however, stories filter down to embarrassments at border posts, police stations and exchange bureaus; of difficulties due to road conditions and spare parts; of high prices in food and accommodation. These are but incidents, surely, to the main purpose of travel which is to see, admire and learn. Baha did have his fair share of problems — immigration officials who were drunk or bribable, police who questioned him at unnecessary length, and so on. Accounts of these have been kept to a minimum. His policy in such circumstances was to be as quiet and patient as possible — his supply of books was large — and then to try and forget all about it. He often failed. Meanwhile, as a guest in a foriegn country, he endeavoured to answer all official questions correctly and, if thereby forced to do so, avoid the black market exchange rates etc..

He did try to live cheaply. By carrying no camera or watch, he had less to worry about and was less obviously the 'rich tourist'. By aiming at a low profile, he hoped to meet more people on as equal a footing as possible. He did not, however, try to live freely. Sometimes, villagers were extremely kind to him but he never tried to live off them. He always carried a tent and food so that, when he stopped in a village for the night, he only needed security from insects, animals and neighbouring tribesmen. Almost invariably he was given this; often much more. If he was given food, he would try to repay in cash or kind. Sometimes he was refused, sometimes he failed to fully appreciate proper values, never was he asked for payment. How easy it is to bring solace to a poor villager. Only a shilling makes all the difference between begrudging and giving, between his rancour and his happiness.

To anyone else who might contemplate a similar trip, the following is suggested: always try to be completely independent in means and never leave a poor family poorer.

For the sake of simplicity, yards have not been converted into metres, the two measurements being approximately the same. And in the book, some distances, methinks, are not quite exact.

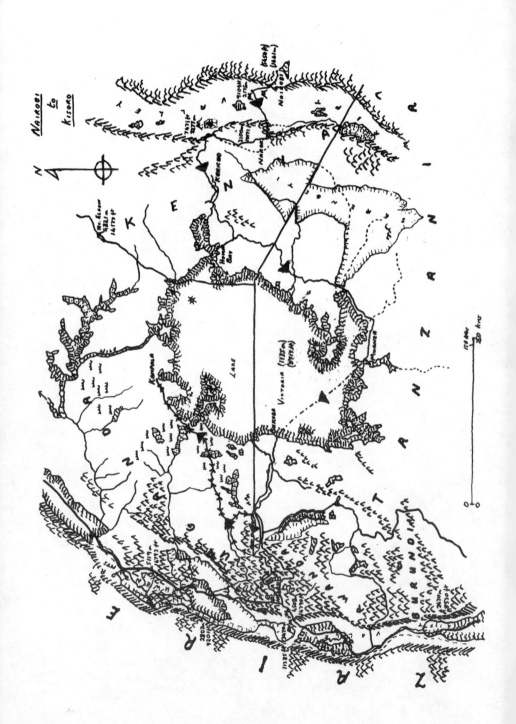

Chapter 1

DEFLATION

In December '73, many people were talking about oil shortages, high petrol prices and the like. (They still are).

"I'll go by bicycle", said Baha to himself, for as usual no-one was listening. Preparations were few, the first happening inadvertently. While endeavouring to get his bike licensed, it was stolen. The problem then was how to get one which would not be highly sought after, for in Nairobi they are precious commodities.

"I'd better get one that nobody wants", he thought, "I'll buy a British export". It was a much lighter machine.

The second preparation was much more difficult – giving up smoking. Then, before finishing his job, he was given a tent and a rucksack but the real decision to undertake the journey was only taken in September. He was unable to arrange a job for himself in the U.K., and so there was thus no reason to rush home, apart from, of course, a love of a mum and a pint of bitter, countered only by a certain dread of the dole. He got out his bicycle. He did not know how far he would go, how long it would take, or how long he would survive with only his own company – most others seemed to get bored with it pretty quickly.

On 17th November, armed with a few visas, he left Nairobi, a city which, to the outsider, looks like any other modern collection of concrete blocks, international advertisements and traffic jams, in which sit, among others, the jet set. The bicycle, loaded with rucksack, tent and tentpoles, was looking a shade odd. Only after a mile or two, therefore, did Baha feel able to put on his rather flowery sunhat. His initial fear had been that he would break down while still within the city, but he was soon happily on the open road in a more traditional Africa; the road climbed up through a very green countryside dotted with many a shamba[1] or farmstead. Each was a self-sufficient home. Huts of mud and thick thatch were on a little space of dried earth, around which were vegetables, maize plants and fruit trees, somewhat spasmodically planted, and amongst them all, chickens and goats competed for morsels. The rolling land was of rich, red soil. Thick patches of numerous greens were separated by the tracks and paths, lines of red where the

1

vegetation had been cleared. These, come the rains, turn to streams . . . red streams which carry the soil miles away, to the hot and arid plains.

The farmland preceded the often coniferous escarpment. From here, at 8,000 feet (approx. 2,500 metres), after looking out across the vast rift valley, he sped downhill. This was rather good, though the faster articulated lorries were a little frightening. Then, however, he left the main road with its busy traffic and started heading across this open valley towards Narok – and now it was lonely, and dead flat. The land stretched for miles to the north and south, its features only varying for the occasional lake or volcanic mountain. On either side stood the longitudinal boundaries of the rift, the escarpments, two steep if not sheer walls of 2,000 feet (600 m) and more, walls separated here by a good 25 miles (40 km), elsewhere by distances in excess of 100 miles (160 km). On the tops were coolness, moisture and greenery; in the valley lay a parched earth. None too healthy grass of a rather dry and light texture surrounded the infrequent small bushes and thorn trees.

There was wild game though nothing ferocious; just gazelle, kongoini (a type of antelope) and the odd giraffe, all of which seemed distinctly surprised to see this sort of human, on two wheels, with a nasty looking bowsprit, suddenly yet quietly appear from down-wind. The value of a bicycle as a hunter's, or better, a photographer's mode of transport seemed proven beyond doubt. Later, rain increased the chances of surprise, though Baha was not pleased to receive his first baptism so soon. His water bottles were still full.

On the other side of the valley was, of course, the other escarpment; so he too had an energy crisis - he was pushing.

2

From behind the odd bush would suddenly appear an occasional Maasai* warrior, armed with spear and rungu (a wooden, knurled club), and wearing just a blanket though his head and arms were often beaded and adorned in red ochre, a dye prepared from the soil.

"Jambo[2] (hallo)" said Baha...quickly. They also wore a smile. At the top of the escarpment, where the vegetation was once more a bit thicker and greener, the tarmac ran out. The road degenerated into a rough track. It was soon obvious that his equipment was totally inadequately secured. Tentpoles and saucepans fell off. Tempers got lost. And the sun was going down. At this stage, Baha felt apprehensive to say the least about sleeping in a Maasai manyatta, a collection of small semi-circular huts around which a fence of thorn tree branches provides protection from wild creatures. He accepted a lift to Narok where he camped and affected many repairs.

In the morning, he made a fresh start on a track which climbed northwards along the edge of the escarpment. Here, amid scenery most tranquil, frequent oaths were heard as buttocks became bruised and loads dislodged. Because of the hilly and rough road, a lot of time was spent pushing rather than peddling. Encouragement was received at one rather muddy point where he pushed slowly yet successfully while others, heading in the other direction, heaved and shoved an expensive four-door, four-wheel and now rather forlorn saloon which sat, nothing on all clocks, in the mud. One advantage of the bicycle was definitely here in its portability. Two large women, cut short in their Sunday afternoon drive, could see only disadvantages in everything, and that included their own physiques. Baha shoved off.

When a mighty rain cloud approached, he decided to forget his earlier apprehensions and to seek shelter in a local homestead. It was a worker's home, a lonely collection of four huts on the edge of a large farming estate. Soon, having pitched his tent, his bruises were forgotten. Now of these huts, three were for the wives – one each; each hut consisted of a kitchen and a bed-cum-living-room. The fourth hut, by far the biggest and best, was for hubby. By tradition, at night, the wives sleep separately in their own huts while the husband decides on which he will bestow his favours. His

---

*A pastoral yet warlike tribe which inhabits much of the rift valley areas of Tanzania and Kenya.

3

host, ministered by these women, sat Baha down by a roaring fire and offered him changaa, an illegal and rather vicious brew. A pleasant evening followed though the kids – dad thought there were about twenty but he'd have to check with the missuses first – were a little noisy. The young girls looked after the babies, leaning way over to the left in order to retain balance while the watoto[3] sat astride the girls' hips under pressure from the right arms. When tired, they would sit the babies upon the dry earth, from where with their large eyes they would scan the world. Rarely would the babies cry. Meanwhile the young boys hoped to emulate dad's promiscuity though at this stage their only contact with the vices was in the running of small erands, collecting more booze or baccy.

Purgatory, the following morning, didn't last very long for the road was soon tarmac again. Once more, he was able to stop concentrating on the road and to look out across that same rift valley where the odd volcanic crater lay dormant, and at the distant hills on the other side. The rich land contained many an occasional shamba[1], some vast areas under corn and, for some incorrigible reason, a lonely English village church built in the Norman style! One presumed that God knew why it was, and still is, in Africa – an old colonial relic no doubt, as out of place as the lions of Longleat. The only cycling problems this day were some undetected friction which delayed even downhill progress, and some girls in a dukah[4] (small shop or kiosk) who wanted to give Baha more than just a cup of chai[5] (tea).

While with friends, Baha bathed his bruises, reduced his load and learnt a bit more about his bicycle. Then on again, westward, over the hills at Kericho where the tea estates stretch seemingly endlessly, towards Lake Victoria. First, he called in to see the shamba[1] of an old acquaintance. This one consisted of but three huts, the husband's having been burnt as part of his funeral service – a tradition which perhaps explains why few of these tribesmen show excessive interest in luxury villas. The main hut, where guests were entertained and men were fed, contained, behind a partition or two, the mother's bed; a second one was a combined kitchen, larder, grannery and henhouse; the last was the son's bedroom and here Baha slept. The water supply was the local and much used stream; the shamba[1] was the widow's only source of livelihood and, for any who passed, a loo.

On a previous visit here, his host, her son, had taken him for a

walk to meet the many neighbouring relatives. In one small hut, he had been entertained to some food; sour milk, cassava and a potent vegetable sat ready on a neat little table. Closer inspection indicated that the latter was early Georgian – another wee relic from those colonial days. The food too had possibly been historic for Baha, within a day, had been stricken low with a vicious diarrhoea. The walk, however, had progressed and had led to the local river for the purposes of a bath. On reaching a quiet spot, the two had stripped off and jumped in. It had only been on surfacing that they had realised they were not alone; on the far bank many a naked maiden was hastily covering herself when she had deciphered the significance of that oddity which was able to proceed upstream – a pair of white buttocks! This time, though, the bath was taken in a small and definitely lonely brook. The day was gloriously warm and Baha decided to read while the waters, murky but nevertheless fresh, flowed over him. His reading was disturbed by what he thought was a bubble of air caught in his crutch. His hand moved to dislodge it. He failed. He tried again. Eventually it – ah! – it was a small eel. Reading was cancelled.

The stay in this shamba[1] was pleasant indeed, for Baha had long since learnt to enjoy a chicken's stomach. Not yet, though, did he enjoy the mosquitoes which become more numerous near Lake

Victoria – blankets as musquito nets tend to be hot and sticky. He thought it odd that so many people, especially among the aged, had lost the six lower front teeth. Apparently, in the old days, these tribesmen had not, unlike most others, practised circumcision. Instead, an individual's adulthood was marked by the crude extraction of these teeth. Imagine – circumcision with a hammer!

Another day's journey took him to Homa Bay on the shores of the big lake*. This was the end of the beginning. He hadn't learnt much really, though he purchased a few more spares before heading down to Tanzania. From here on, he was alone in what was, to him, the unknown. In the hilly countryside, spasmodically bejewelled by the sun reflecting off the few corrugated iron roofs which were replacing the traditional thatch, many a pipe smoking woman busied herself. Frequently, little streams bubbled towards the lake, bouncing over the pebbles and . . . oh, sorry . . . a stream is often a bath. After some miles (some more kms), he stopped in a local market to take his first drink, uji, a sort of unsweetened porridge of millet served in a gourd; 'twas heavy, bitter and very filling. The African market is a hubble of life: colours, in cereals, vegetables, fruit and clothes abound, either in the stalls or just simply laid out on the ground in front of their owner who sits, patiently, perhaps all day, waiting to sell. Animals wander unfettered. Occasionally women argue; usually there is such a high level of cheerful noise that these events remain undetected.

He spent the first night in a little shamba[1] where conversation was difficult. Usually, but not this time, this was because of Baha's poor Swahili. Here, a rather remote area, his host knew only his own tribal tongue. The old farmer, who thought Baha was at least fifty because of his beard, invited him into his own bedroom for the night – the wife, just the one, stayed in her own hut with the kids, just the two. In between the two huts were kept, by night, the family fortunes, a small herd of cows. There they rested with maximum security, safe from wild animals, cattle raiders and other beef speculators. Before going to sleep, Baha was shown a collection of spears, knives, bows and arrows which the old boy kept on the wall within constant reach from his bed. And under his pillow was one very special dagger. Hoping he wouldn't sleep walk, Baha dozed off.

---

* Big? Let's have a look. Now the biggest lake in the British Isles must be Lough Neagh. Well, Lake Victoria is not only bigger than Lough Neagh; it is also bigger than Ulster. Indeed, it's bigger than Ulster, Leinster and Munster put together!

Little dukahs[4] are not so numerous in Tanzania and chances of stopping for a quick cup of chai[5] were now few. From here on there was no fresh milk. Bread was a luxury found only in the infrequent towns. The roads too were not good, but often nearby there was a little path smoothed by the pressures of countless bare feet. Here, cycling was much easier than on the rough and rutted highway. One such pair of feet belonged to a young mother who was returning, her baby on her back, with her shopping carried on top of her head. It stood, on end, perfectly still, for only the hips and legs were moving. The day's purchases were but one - just a small tin of baby powder – ah . . . progress. Meanwhile, Baha's own progress, because of the odd puncture, was slow. He was glad to be invited in by a farmer's wife for the night. He pitched tent near a line of drying fish and was then given a good meal followed by a pleasant chat, all sitting on the hard, dry and well brushed earth around the evening fire. Each home is surrounded by such a patch of dead soil as a precaution against insects and snakes. 'Tis not so good when it rains.

The staple food is ugali[6] which, like mealie meal, is prepared from maize. The cobs' seeds are placed in a deep wooden bowl on the ground. Then, armed with a long pole, women of mighty bicep pound the defenceless vegetable until all its skins are shed. Afterwards, all is repeatedly flung in the air. That which lands back in the banana leaf tray is good, while the husks are carried away by the wind to the waiting chickens. It then has to be ground before cooking, when the women's muscles are tested again, for the putty-like food needs constant turning with the large wooden spoon that may be up to two feet (60 cms) long. The finished product arrives as a large, smooth, dense hemisphere which is then eaten by hand, and by mouth, usually with another plate of a meat or vegetable stew. Ugali[6] is an acquired taste; acquired, Baha thinks, by having little else to choose from.

The journey continued, sometimes over hills, sometimes, despite the lake's proximity, across hot, open, dry, flat plains. By the time he arrived at the next village, he was often pretty tired and hungry. So, well tired anyway, was the bike. Once he sat and sighed over a drink, only to see it also offer a small sigh and sink a little towards the ground – yet another puncture! Often, he received help from other cyclists. A certain fraternity seemed to exist among such two-wheeled travellers, rather like the thumbs-up clubs among

7

veteran sports-car enthusiasts. On many occasions, Baha was assisted with his punctures, and accompanied on the road. Rarely was he able to reciprocate help, though once he managed to lend his pump. And thus he was invited to another home. After a small walk through banana and cassava plantations, the two had a swim in the roughish waters of Lake Victoria, hippos and bilhertzia* rumoured to be elsewhere. It was odd to see large waves a' breaking, not on a beach, but on a cabbage plot. Later, they sat round a dung fire while the womenfolk gracefully served, first water in which all washed their hands, and then food before withdrawing backwards with many curtseys to leave the men eating alone - the father of the family was a former chief.

At Mwanza, Baha bought many spare tubes – he had learnt his first lesson – before catching the overnight boat to Bukoba. Crowds piled on and soon he felt obliged to offer his seat to a woman who had three kids with her, the youngest of which was still being breast fed. So he sat on the deck where, later, he was offered some food. It was a kind gesture but, because of eating communally, as is their custom, with the two other hungry children, he achieved little.

After a hard and noisy night (there was, as ever, at least one shauri[7] or argument which woke everybody) sleeping where he sat, the boat, with the dawn, came to the shore. He cycled up into the hills leaving many pleasant views of the lake behind him. Here, probably because of the recent Uganda/Tanzania political tension, some people were not too friendly. At the border town, dubious looks were cast at the beard, many questions were repeatedly asked and everything was laboriously searched. After such treatment, Baha was determined to get well away from these police and to move on to the next village for the night, but it was already late. Soon he was in completely open country, passing through a sugar cane estate into virgin bush not far from a sizeable river. The sun was down but this next village, according to the map, was not too far ahead. However, progress on the sandy road was slow. There were many fairly large bushes on this grassy rolling countryside. It looked like buffalo country but, mercifully, there were none. It looked like stalking country too but . . . The moon was up, casting many eerie shadows. He felt not a little worried. The droppings he saw were probably of cows but he wasn't sure

---

*A snail, often found in still waters, from which a disease of the same name is caught.

8

whether or not other equally large yet fiercer animals left similar signs. What dubious professional qualifications he possessed were not in this field. He looked for signs of lights but all he saw were many flashing phosphorescent insects which teased his imagination incessantly. It was dark, empty and lonely. Then, the final straw, he got another puncture, his fifth of the day – such were the habits of his stop-go cycle. He paused to panic, but just then a land-rover luckily came along and carried him the one remaining mile to the village. It was good to see people, friendly ones. The mosquitoes were anything but. Baha – later, retrospectively, he felt very stupid – had neither repellent nor net; he was severely bitten. He slept little; he tried putting his head outside the tent leaving all of them inside; he switched on his torch and hurled it into the bush; he tried curling up in his sleeping bag but the sweat was too much; he tried instant prayer. All his tactics were in vain. He swore, and impatiently waited for the dawn.

The road into Uganda was again lonely – there was one little group of igloo-shaped huts, barely four feet (1.2 m) high, the inhabitants of which wore animal skins; a few huts elsewhere sported tin roofs and were more definitely in the twentieth century. The road was sandy. This meant fewer punctures but more pushing; at times, where it was especially thick, he was even pushing downhill. Once, suddenly, he stopped. There, not far ahead of him,

an enormous pair of horns, some five feet (1.5 m) across, was coming out of the bush. His heart beat faster, his jaw dropped, he began to sweat. He felt not just a little stupid when the rest of the animal appeared – it was a cow. No letters home for that one.

Shortly afterwards, Baha was welcomed to Uganda – by a signpost. There wasn't a soul anywhere though the land, judging by the knee-high grass, was fertile; a river flowed nearby and beyond was a commanding range of hills. The world was not looking over-populated. To the north, he later learnt, settlement had been started with a few Rwandan refugees. After some miles riding up the river valley, he reached a little village, reported to the police and made his presence legal; and, in so doing, interrupted one constable's quiet, Saturday afternoon, duty booze-up. Then he aimed for a mission; this would give him a chance to wash himself and his clothes, and to pray in the morning for another week's good fortune. The padre said Baha was brave to be alone in Uganda – brave or stupid. Before sleeping, he recollected how on a previous visit to Uganda, he had found himself for the first time at the wrong end of a British rifle, held rather vaguely yet menacingly to his abdomen by some scruffy soldier.

The local countryside was now hillier and more populated, though it was difficult to see the small houses, surrounded as they were by many huge banana plants. These provide the basic food-stuff, matoke, which arrives on one's plate, again after much pounding and beating, as a fairly solid, orange mass. Its taste was favourable; better, Baha thought, than that of the Kenyan ugali[6]. A second difference in Uganda was the smell, a smell which got stronger as each day progressed, the potent odour of pombe[8], the local beer. There were no chai[5] dukahs[4], so he drank just water; much was now needed as he pushed the bike, once more on tarmac, up into the hills which precede, yet again, the rift valley. In a town, there were dukahs[4] enough. During his meal, a car containing four, open-eyed, open-mouthed Africans drove slowly past. All eight eyes scanned Baha, the only mzungu[10] (European) in sight and, because he was white, he was automatically suspect.

"That's intelligence", the landlord whispered.

'Twas a good disguise.

Back in the country, drunkards were many. He was grateful to choose, quite by chance, a teetotaller as host for the night; hospitality, as so often happened, was overwhelming. Instead of pitching his tent in the shamba[1], Baha and his bicycle were invited in to sleep in the sitting room. A pleasant conversation in English followed (Swahili is not so popular in Uganda) while a bevy of offspring offered drinks of sour milk, understood little, but giggled a lot. The next morning, as he set off once more along the valley road, he was challenged to a race by a happy fellow pushing a wheelbarrow. The latter soon retired, hurt perhaps, drunk certainly, and definitely outdistanced. Two wheels, of course, are better than one.

During the previous evening, his host had warned of the immensity of these hills.

"First", he said, "you'll have to walk for about five miles (8 km). Then, later on, you will reach a second range necessitating another, longer push".

"He's unfit", thought Baha quietly. In the early morning mist which hung onto the numerous tall trees, he was unable to see the size of the obstacle. The road slowly twisted and curled its way up into the mountains. He rose with the mist, and soon he was looking back down into the valley with its sinuous river. Later, when the mist had completely cleared, he saw many ranges of hills separated by lakes or rich, green, alluvial plains, both of which snaked their way in search of lower altitudes. The hillsides were covered in small plots where much varied agriculture took place and, by the look of things, had been doing so for centuries. Each little plot was in one stage or another of cultivation, a few perhaps were just fallow. Each had its own colour – greens, yellows and browns were permutated by time – all constituted one large, magnificent, vegetable mosaic. (On these steep slopes, tractors would be useless. 'Development' tends to cause the depopulation of such areas. It's sad to see excellent systems becoming obsolescent). The natural beauty, enhanced by this quiltwork, was overpowering. Baha stopped, sat, got out his sketch pad which a hopeful friend had given him, and started. His patience, alas, was insufficient.

He moved on, into a thick bamboo forest. And there, on the other side, was, in Baha's opinion, the most beautiful view of the entire journey. The land, with the forest behind, dropped away into another quiltwork of hills and vales overlooking Kisoro to the west, while to the south, it rose again, up into three mighty volcanic peaks whose heads were in the clouds. 'Twas fantastic.

"Who, with a small farm on these hillsides, with such a home

11

in which lie a wife, a child, a transistor and an aspirin, who wants change?"

He was reluctant to leave such beauty but he had to, for food if nothing else. His last meal had been some twenty-four hours earlier. He bumped and thus descended, and later entered the crowded streets of Kisoro to look for both a police station, where he had to report before going to Zaire, and a dukah[4]. His eyes wandered. Bang! He collided with one of many pedestrians who was so aghast at the sight of Baha plus bike that he ran off in terror, leaving his basket of shopping neatly hanging on the tentpoles. Only through an intermediary could a return of goods be effected.

After a large meal, he went to the police. Initially, all welcomed him; later a senior official decided this (this? what this?) was not good enough. Baha was arrested and told to sleep on the police station floor. From an adjacent cell, the shrieking voice of an old woman cried in vain for freedom. He slept little, his imagination less. His only pleasantry was a small meal of fried grasshoppers – they were very good, having a taste half way between those of shrimps and cornflakes.

Thus Baha went back through these same beautiful hills but somehow their beauty, from inside a bumpy country bus, was not so inspiring. The destination, reached twenty-four hours later, was Kampala police headquarters, and here he was threatened with deportation. This was the last thing he wanted. He said a silent prayer or two, called everybody 'sir', and hoped. And his only hope was to regard such an impossible situation, like many a God-fearing African does, as a 'shauri[7] ya Mungu' (all part of God's plan).

And, while Baha languishes in Ugandan police stations awaiting dubious decision-making processes, perhaps I should tell you a little bit about him.

He was part of the war time effort, arriving on the English scene in '43. And some effort it must have been, for most had thought he would be two – but no, just one large one, which was then dieted in order to give him a more stable growth pattern. The first incident of note occurred near the end of the war when he was sitting in his pram, quietly perusing the Times crossword or a rattle – his memory is vague – when a rogue dog bit him. For years, he feared animals, dogs let alone elephants.

At a small monastic school, he was a quiet lad, passing with nauseating frequency most exams which contrasted with his

12

complete lack of success when armed with a cricket bat. He cherished the thought of joining the Navy for some unknown reason probably inherited from his hard working, conventional mum. His more peaceful father died when Baha was but a lad, so the Navy it was to be. A dotted line was signed in complete ignorance, and off he went to Dartmouth, that well known, nautical sausage factory. Baha became a short and plump sausage, but accent and bearing were regulation, and his taste for beer and birds conformed to his new society. But he was much more successful with booze than he was with the blondes.

And so to sea, as a submariner. A good life, where the most expensive games are played at someone else's expense, but where a sense of equality is strong, for all share the same food, the same cramped conditions, the same stink as yet again the slop drain and sewage tank is vented inboard. After one or two hair-raising moments in his second boat, which could have led to a court martial, he settled down to become an above average naval officer, as his 'chitty' said, but thereagain, so did everybody else's.

But enough of this, he thought. In 1970, having seen the poverty of the world in the Far East and elsewhere, he resigned, turned down a university offer, and started to teach as a volunteer in Kenya – here was his own small contribution to the third world. His first lesson was hell; he spoke shakily, he didn't know his subject and all his African pupils looked alike. His subject – new maths. First impressions were that it was to a large extent unsuited to English kids, let alone Africans. Three and a half years later, his pupils took 'O' levels and achieved record results, but those initial impressions still remained. What did change, however, was Baha. Slowly, the old yachting blazer disintegrated and his 'British rhubarb' attitude altered to one more egalitarian in spirit. He donned a pair of flip-flops, bought a bicycle and started to learn Swahili. He began to respect the African, to understand his way.

Baha also taught physics, and outside the lab there now appeared a shanti, a few homes of cardboard and polythene for some poor folk who had been moved on by the authorities. "Jambo", Baha would say on his way to a lesson. A most cheerful mama smiled her reply, a beautiful daughter caught his eye; a relationship built up, via help when the authorities burnt all their polythene, via a cycle ride behind the black maria which took them all to a police station because some politician was due to visit the school. Some staff protested, and the rift between Baha and the mzungu[10] headmaster widened further. Contact was maintained with the shanty folk however, and a visit to their shamba[1] followed. This, combined with two other visits to boys' up-country homes gave Baha his first real insight into African life . . . plus a mild form of dysentry. It is, afterall, quite possible to stay in Kenya for years, playing golf and sipping gin, without really learning anything about the African traditions. Only now was Baha starting.

This introduction, however, combined with a dislike of returning home just to become another unemployment statistic, gave him the confidence to attempt this reasonably formidable cycle ride. And somehow, something had moved him to get all those necessary visas and so on. It had all appeared to be working to that sort of plan. But perhaps not, he now thought, as he laid out his sleeping bag on the hard table for another night in the uncertain company of armed Ugandan bobbies.

Eventually he was allowed to stay – he never did discover an offence and nor did his captors, though General (now Field Marshall or more) Amin had apparently decreed that tourists ·should only enter Uganda by air or directly from Kenya, even if other borders were open (thus, presumably, he hoped to get the rich ones). Now what the President decreed, all obeyed. Few could foretell what the next inspired order would be; it seemed to depend on random factors like which side of bed he had got out of that morning, and which wife had been in. Baha's only punishment was a major one: the compulsory loss of his beard – at his own cost! Three years' hard work ruined. On consideration, the punishment could have been worse – only his facial hair was considered offensive. One senior policeman was actually disappointed for he had thought Baha to be a prophet.

And so, after two nights on police station tables and one on a bus station bench, he was escorted back to Kisoro. Life in the bus station was difficult, especially for the women in their large, billowing, semi-Victorian dresses; they carried children on their backs and balanced loads on their heads. In such crowded situations, it would normally be the bundles which would suffer, yet somehow, heads twisted and twirled, and collisions were rare.

During these five days under arrest, he read all his books and mended over a dozen punctures. The books he now sold and thereby acquired funds with which to buy a razor and such like heavy stores. He was not ill-treated, though they sometimes forgot to feed him. Matoke, that banana pulp, had in these parts competition from an imported food, locally called 'Irish potatoes'. Most Ugandans were quite pleasant. Some of the police were sympathetic though a certain William could not understand Baha's logic when he suggested that his days under police scrutiny had achieved nothing positive and that, therefore, they were equivalent to five days of death. An exceptional copper was far from kind; he remains vividly in Baha's memory; this particular policeman, not perhaps surprisingly rather an ugly specimen whose face basically needed reshuffling and dealing again, threatened Baha with a whip! Fortunately, his excort saved the day.

Ugandan country buses were quite unique. On this return journey, the bus left Kampala twelve hours late. It was completely packed (as a general rule, nothing moved until it was at least full), and, half way home, it suddenly changed its route for the convenience of a few. Nobody objected, perhaps because the permanent noise level was high if not overpowering. Boisterous men competed with thirsty babies, tired kids and undisciplined chickens. One could sing to oneself in perfect oblivion - it was nice to hear Tchaikovsky again. Later, there was a police check to make sure there was no overcrowding. Perhaps, however, the copper had only had a primary education. He gave up.

Baha and bicycle were taken in a police pick-up on the last leg to Kisoro, again, and then the border. As always, the government vehicle was also used by an occasional civilian or two, probably some of the driver's undoubtedly numerous relatives. In front was a mama and her two little children. Because she was trying to breast feed one, Baha offered to hold the elder. He settled the mtoto[3] into what he thought was a comfortable position though the rough road didn't help. Immediately – he had obviously been most successful – a little hand climbed up Baha's chest, undid a shirt button and nipped inside for a nipple. The child's disappointment at finding only a few scraggly hairs was readily apparent. He reluctantly decided to sleep but somehow, he never quite got over his unquenched thirst. Later, as Baha looked for the last time at those three majestic volcanoes, the little fellow vomitted – all over him – disaster. Mother was most apologetic.

"Don't worry", said Baha after a change of shirt, "he couldn't help it. You cannot blame a child for something so natural; you can

15

only blame adults for mistakes, like the arresting of innocent cyclists". The policeman remained silent.

His Ugandan visit was now at an end. He had learnt to believe no word until the act promised was completed. So near had he been to ill-administered discipline that Baha began to put faith in the advice an old man in Nairobi had given him prior to his departure – "Go with God".

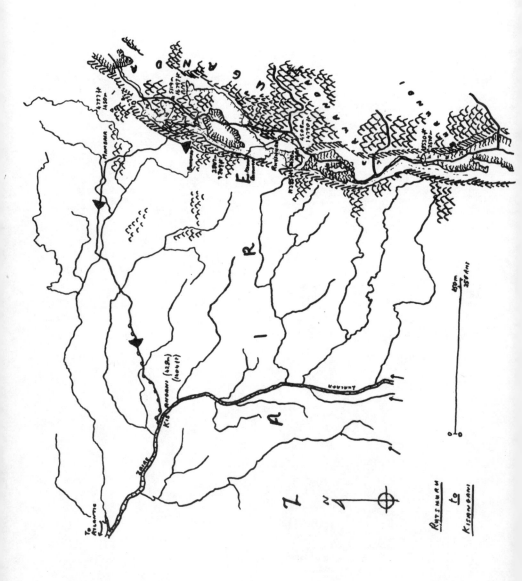

Chapter 2.

OFF.

He was deposited on the Zairois border at 5 o'clock on a Saturday evening. In Uganda, he had had ample time to read one of those 'how to learn French without really trying' books but, alas, the only word he understood when the immigration official delivered a lengthy speech was 'visa'. (French for visa is visa.) Life in Zaire might be difficult, he thought, but after Uganda it was heaven and anyway, turning back was impossible.

Fortunately, Rutshuru was not far away and there, after some assistance from an army lorry which picked him up out of the night, he found a mission – well, almost heaven. He tried again to speak French, this time to a Belgian priest, for this would be less embarrassing. He thought up a sentence, strolled up confidently, caught the man's attention and opened his mouth. Nothing came out. Nothing! After a moment or two, he had to admit complete defeat and ask, meekly: "Do you speak English?" An answer came and comforted. He pitched tent. Later he learnt that Eastern Zairois speak Swahili – he was saved.

In the morning, he started his sojourn in Zaire properly. Life was a little confusing for the numbers on the milestones (kilokilometregrams?) went up, not down. Not only did these Francophones drive on the wrong side of the road but also, it seemed, they went backwards. Via Swahili, he started picking up and practicing French, usually with school-boys for most adults preferred their traditional tongue. Sometimes, these practice lessons got no further than a couple of French jambo's[2]. He also conversed, somewhat one-sidedly but definitely in French, with some local flies which had taken an unwanted fancy to this sweating cyclist. He pedalled faster, hoping to achieve more than fly speed and thereby part company. But in vain. His sweat increased, as did the number of these insects which relished this human plus sauce, salt added.

From Rutshuru he headed north and soon came to the entrance of a game park. The game wardens, amid chuckles, handed him the usual instruction sheet which read "Ne quittez pas le piste et restez

dans votre voiture" ("Don't leave the track and stay in your car").
After a few Swahili jokes, they watched him go down through the
gate, over a bridge and into the bush. He was soon alone on a rough
road which carved its way through the many trees. Signposts
merely warned of elephants; they gave no advice. However, at this
stage, he saw only a few baboon, and they quickly disappeared.

A few miles further on, the road ran alongside a broad river.
There were hippos everywhere, some quietly swimming, others
making a terrible din, all in or near the water. At one point, there
was a mighty commotion taking place though, amidst all the
splashes, he saw only one hippo's head. What the other fighter was
he never learnt for, by the time he had braked to a halt and walked
back into view, it was all over. It did cause him to think, though, of
his own non-existent weapons of self-defence.

A little later on, when rounding a corner, he saw, about 30
yards ahead of him, two hippos on dry land within 4 yards of the
road. He stopped. The size of the problem was immediately
apparent. Silence reigned. His thumping heart was in his mouth.
He stood still. Pause.

"Now according to the rules, I am meant to stay on the track
and hippos are supposed to remain in the water, for they normally
only come out to eat by night," he thought. It didn't help. He stopped
thinking, and waited. Slowly, the two mighty beasts walked
towards other grass nearer the river. When they were about 10
yards from the road, he tired of waiting, remounted and cycled
quietly past. They noticed and turned their heavy heads towards,
but mercifully decided that grass was better than Baha. He resumed
breathing.

All the others were in the gently flowing river and this sight
alone was well worth admiring. The road, however, was still rough.
At one stage, he thought he heard a small hiss of air.

"Blast. Another puncture." He stopped, and dismounted to
investigate. There, directly behind him and about 70 yards away,
was a lone buffalo looking straight at him. Quickly, very quickly, he
decided he didn't have a puncture, remounted and shot off as fast as
his two wheels would carry him. Normally, on confronting a beast,
one should stand absolutely still, but there wasn't much point in
attempting arborial disguise on this occasion for two reasons; trees
don't move first and only then stand still, nor do they ride bicycles.
The buffalo hissed again.

Soon the road left the river and rose onto a large open plain. He stopped, relaxed, and turned to look back at the scene of his recent excitement. There, invisible from the lower road because of bush, was the largest herd of elephant and buffalo he had ever seen!

Now, however, life was much better. On these grassy plains were the more docile impala and gazelle, and even one or two peaceful people. He got that puncture. Later, at the only lodge, he had a beer. Time for rest was short though, as there was still a good distance to go and he did not wish to be caught in the park after dark. At first, he was still on the plains viewing some idle buck and, at a comfortable distance, a large but contented herd of buffalo. Then he started to climb; he was across the rift valley and meeting yet another escarpment. Behind it, the sun was going down and the dusk was obviously going to be early and long. The animals started to make noises for now was their time for sport; and Baha started pushing. Gradually, the mountain's shadow swallowed him. Along the path were some large feline tracks and, though his imagination, after the morning's episode, was working vividly, he only saw little monkeys, a few squirrels and one charming rat. Rarely before has such a rodent looked so harmless and angelic.

Perhaps his own tracks, two foot and two wheel prints, would cause fierce arguments and many nasal twitches. From the other side of a nearby hill, he heard a very loud and ugly noise – its owner was obviously large and mobile, though it remained hidden. It sounded rather like an addicted elephant with a bad, bronchial, smoker's cough. It repeated itself often, this base vibration from the bottom of some pretty deep throat (some chicken!) but each time, it had moved to the new opposite side of this little hill. The day ended with a tired Baha approaching the park gate, with the sun's rays fading behind the hills, and with some very unfriendly looks from a lone buffalo bull. Fortunately, a gorge kept him at bay. At the gate, Baha was allowed to camp with the game warden. Over a fire, he explained about this enormous noise he had heard.

"C'était le guerille (that was a gorilla)" was the warden's reply, but Baha wasn't sure. And he'll never learn.

Come the dawn, he cycled the short distance to the little village of Kanyabayonga where he stopped for a meal. 'Kanyabayonga for breakfast'; it sounded rather good. But no; for a long time in some little dukah[4] there was an unpalatable silence, later, a little rice and veg. Afterwards, however, mobile once more, there was something

21

positive to admire: the road climbed up through rows of trees amidst rich and fertile undulating farmland. The mud houses, both in the villages and fields, looked very smart with their thick thatch, while their walls were painted with an earth dye to give them that dual-tone touch. The villages were really very pretty. They usually consisted of just two lines of these little square huts facing each other across the road. In the country, lines of eucalyptus made superb avenues which overlooked many a quiet pastoral scene or large area of virgin undergrowth. Presumably, these trees had been planted by Belgian settlers, of whom the only reminders were the empty and crumbling brick farmsteads.

In one village where he stopped for a quick egg, a somewhat rare commodity in these parts, a mighty procession passed through. A coffin was carried in front of many gaily dressed women who sang happily for the deceased. It was a good way to go. Baha followed, at a distance.

The road continued to climb. At home one can cycle up a hill in an hour or two, but this mighty lot took almost all day. The views, now less agricultural as the road approached hills of virgin forest, were reward enough. And it was pleasant, he thought, to be away from animals. Numerous little children in the various villages along the way had taken over, crying "Touriste, touriste." This got Baha a little annoyed – time to learn another French word! At one stage, while mending a puncture, he did practice 'son français' with a passer-by and managed a tolerable conversation. Having finished, he remounted, smiled, waved, and bid him a cheerful "Aujourd'hui."

The look he got as the sole reply was most perplexed and unhappy. Only later did Baha remember that the word for good-bye was not 'aujourd'hui', but 'au revoir'. Nearly right.

The next day brought him to the downhill side of the mountains, where the road sinusoidally bumped its tortuous way through thick woodland. Though often in lonely parts, he still felt fairly safe from the point of view of animals. Once, however, he revised his opinion: on stopping for a pee by the side of the road, the tree in front of him suddenly became alive with squeaking monkeys which rapidly disappeared, somewhat distressed by such blatant bad manners. And every evening, swallows in their hundreds, all perhaps British exports, zoomed above the jungle trees in several directions at once in search of insects – or telegraph poles?

22

Food was becoming a bit of a problem. Even in a large town like Butembo, little was available. It was interesting to see, however, a really positive attempt at African urbanisation; the residential parts of town were traditional village huts, now laid out in a street formation. It was a bit too rectangular possibly, but so much more practical than Europeanised development. To return to the more important item, food; once, a meal was one complete pineapple. Delicious. He had the same for supper. Thus, feeling now a little sick, he went off pineapples. On another occasion, in the middle of nowhere, he found a sign marked 'boulangerie'. In the little hut behind, he was offered a choice of bread, eggs, chai[5] or beer. Later, he left, no longer hungry, just confused as to the meaning of that sign. That night, the confusion deepened. He stopped in a small roadside village where, as far as about fifty kids were concerned, he was the cause of some curiosity. Dad eventually sent them away. During the night he awoke – he had caught a sudden dose of diarrhoea. Time was short; he rushed out of the hut, looked, panicked, crossed the road and had a quick george over the bank. Later, a second attack forced him to perform an action replay. By this time, however, the first light of dawn was just beginning to appear and chaps were inclined to get up rather early in these parts. An old man gracefully passed by on the other side of the road.

Dawn meant possible further embarrassment, so he left straight away although, because of the forest and altitude, it was misty and cool. The sound of running water – always so pleasant when impersonal – assured him of further downhill cruising. The road kept close to this little river which forced its way through a narrow, rocky gorge. A second embarrassment did occur, but it was small. A group of young women, wearing long multi-coloured dresses and carrying loads on their heads, were gracefully walking to market. The backs were straight and steady; under them, the hips wobbled and the skirts in sympathy rippled. Baha, from behind, wished to come through. Having no bell, he made a hearty cry:

"We!"* he shouted. (In Swahili slang, it means 'hey you' but, as a general rule, it seems to convey that meaning everywhere.) All, amid falling loads and feminine squeals, immediately scattered, some diving into the bush despite complete ignorance of what they

---

* pronounced 'Whey!'

would land on. Graceful was no longer a suitable adjective, even with those who were now horizontal.

"I knew I should have kept my beard."

Later, he reached the edge of the forest overlooking a magnificent view of the Zaire river basin. A mass of vegetation disappeared in all directions westward unto the horizon. He descended the last remaining thousand feet or so and entered. The road was poor; only with poetic license could this jungle be given the adjective 'drive-in'. No longer were there great views over fantastic distances; because of all the trees, one could see no further than a few yards. This vegetation though was impressive in its own right. There were trees whose trunks rose vertically for eighty feet (24m) or so before bursting into branch and leaf, while below there were palms, giant bracken and numerous other plants . . . and many long-winded words found in encyclopedias. Every so often, the jungle had been cleared and therein stood a roadside village amidst a little cultivated land. In front of the little wooden houses was at least one separate building rather like a bus shelter, a 'baraza[9] hut', the one communal building. Here, if the sun was too hot, the rain too heavy, or the night too lonely, one could come for comfort or company. Indeed one could, weather permitting as it were, spend one's entire life there, resting and doing nothing . . . . if one was a man.

Several had good cause to rest at this time of year for there were frequent heavy showers. Between the huts, little streams quickly formed in what had been a solid earth surface. It soon became a quagmire. In the shelter of their overhanging roofs, families waited for the rain to pass, though some were still collecting their cassava which, up until a few seconds earlier, had been drying in the sun. These little streams made their way into the road. Both sides were soon quite full; the convex road became an island; the water was red with the soil it carried; the streams only left the roadside and entered the jungle at the bottom of each rise. If the rain fell at an angle, it tended to take away a bit of each hut's mud wall, unless their overhanging roofs were sufficiently broad. These, if thatch, could only survive a year or two of tropical storms; if corrugated, they would last much longer though the sanity of their owners would become suspect – inside, they are incredibly noisy. The rain would go, often as quickly as it had come. The sun would reappear and all soon would return to normal; it didn't take long for a village compound area, so recently a mud bath, to become terra firma* once more.

Earlier, Baha had received advice against taking the road. Towards the end of the day, he began to understand – the road had become little more than a track. However, so far was so good and, as a cyclist, he rarely contemplated turning back. He camped in a tiny village of but four huts. In pitching tent, he experienced considerable difficulty when trying to bang his pegs into the hard ground, but in the still of the tropical evening, he decided all was adequately secured. One hut was a tiny little dukah[4] and he was able to buy a tin or two of sardines. The owner was obviously delighted with this record turnover – '73? . . . . a good year.

And thus, he resolved to sleep under the stars. After a quiet read, he rolled to rest. But something went wrong. The stars went out. One of the neighbours woke him, warned of yet more approaching rain and offered solid shelter in his own home. This Baha declined, disappointed in the landlord's lack of confidence with the camping arrangements. The kind man parted, and went back to his own bed.

The noise grew louder, the wind stronger, and then, bang, the rain fell. It was heavy. The tent started to leak but, ah, it wasn't serious. Most of the water was left outside. He rearranged his polythene, thought that where there was cloud there would be sun, and tried once more to sleep. Further leaks started. It was coming down in buckets. Like an exhausted ostrich, he moved his head further into the depths of his sleeping bag in the hope of sleep and pleasant, albeit lubricated dreams. Ah . . . . zizz; he rolled gently and thought idly. But dampness, in the manner of a mating octopus, came at him from all directions. His patience was fading. Then, after a sudden and really rather unnecessary gust of wind, the sodden tent collapsed.

Most people at this stage would be tempted to lose their sense of humour. Baha lost his temper. Soaked, he now was. He knocked on the landlord's door but, alas, they were sound asleep. There was a small 'baraza[9] hut' nearby and here he got tolerable though damp shelter for the rest of the night.

"One advantage of travelling alone was that no-one of

---

* solid ground.

permanence called you an idiot". He slept, with some humility and much humidity.

Sure enough, the next morning, the sun was shining, though it took a long time to get everything dry. On leaving, he passed over a bridge and from there until another bridge some forty miles (64 kms) later, the road was astrocious. Parallel ruts showed that vehicles had used it in days gone by, but the jungle had long since started to reclaim possession. Riding along the central island was extremely difficult - it was thin and bumpy, and visibilty was reduced by the grass and general vegetation which plagued his eyes! (May I assure the reader that Baha was still the right way up). Maintaining balance was the biggest problem and often he struggled in vain. Because of the narrow island between the two deep ruts, he couldn't stop and dismount without inflicting on the crossbar severe inconvenience to his crutch. It was better, on losing balance, to admit defeat, realise the gravity of the situation, and stay on the saddle until both Baha and the bike lay horizontal in the bush. Frequently did he start off only to fall off. The fear of a thorny landing, or even a live one, tormented him, but the only creatures he disturbed were ants. The disturbance was instantly more than mutual; pants, as rumoured, have disadvantages. The day was not enhanced by the odd rain shower, several patches of thick mud and the occasional puncture. In the evening, he was entertained by a family who lived in their very own part of the jungle in almost total isolation – splendid; resting over a dish of peanut soup and a glass of pombe[8], he realised that he had only covered twenty miles (32 kms) that day.

"Do cars ever use this road?" An emphatic, Swahili 'no way' was the sole reply. On Baha's map, the cartographer had coloured it in red; he should really have used a faint and foggy pencil, for the wretched thing was definitely no more than a track suitable only for olympic kangaroos.

The next day saw the road gradually get better, there being no other alternative. Life was a good deal more pleasant, though a kind offer of native honey, in which the dead bees co-existed with their life-time's souvenirs, ensured more rumblings from the gut. In one little village, he stopped to buy a paw-paw and received instead a welcome into the 'baraza hut', from the ceiling of which hung many bunches of fruit for over a year before they were used to make pombe[8]. Here, he was offered a smoke from a pipe over six feet

26

(1.8m) long. It is indeed difficult, but even in the tropics not impossible, to get that cool smoke. Later, he met some hunters who pursued duikers and other animals with bows, arrows and nets. The only wild life seen, however, were hosts of many and varied butterflies all of which appeared to live off the dung of various animals which littered the road. It seemed a pity that such beauty should thrive on and off such excrement, though at times, he thought, they showed rather better taste by flying in formation for a yard or few, positioning themselves just a couple of inches in front of his nose. Further on he saw for the first time some Pygmies; the curiosity was mutual though a bit unbalanced. Some of their women wore next to nothing, next to something. They were a friendly people who, it seemed, were permanently happy. Their way of life was similar to that of other jungle dwellers; some food was hunted, most was grown. Life's tastes were few, and therefore so too were life's problems.

As the sun went down, its last rays playing with intricate delicacy among the colours and the shadows of the trees, a tired Baha arrived at Mambasa. Earlier, two fellow cyclists had been shocked beyond words to see a cycling mzungu[10] come down this particular track. He went to the mission where he hoped to pitch his tent. Initially, he had to wait. He settled down with his book under an outside light run from a nearby generator. As the evening drew on, insects arrived from everywhere to plague the innocent bulb. Reading soon became nigh on impossible until suddenly, some hungry ducks waddled speedily in the direction of all this meat. His relaxation continued, though many a gobbling duck's beak attacking moths which had endeavoured to seek refuge in the hairs of his legs, tended to decrease the literary intake. The day finished on a superb note – a bed.

Now his back wheel had just about had enough of these rough roads; some cracks in the rim were looking serious. There were no spares anywhere but, at this mission, he was luckily able to get a spot of welding done. He then thought it would be an intelligent move to swop rims so that the weaker wheel would be at the front under a lighter load. Thus the entire day was spent in messing around with spokes; he learnt first that the front wheel had fewer spokes and that therefore a swop was impossible, and secondly that to spoke a wheel, a definite pattern was necessary.

In the morning he was back on the main road, though it was

still badly rutted for the first few miles. Progress was slow, and the back wheel was none too happy. Potholes abounded, though some of these because they were so enormous he could manage quite easily – like a cork masters that which a ship considers a dangerous wave. Food was also still a problem. Dukahs[4] were few and rarely did cooking take place by day because the women were invariably at work in the shamba[1]. Their one cooked meal was supper. So Baha's hunger was usually satisfied by the purchase of fruit from the menfolk in the little villages. One such village was called Banana and only that foodstuff was available; but never before has he seen bananas so huge – a good foot (30 cms) long and proportionately thick. They were bright yellow, rather sweet and very filling. One was a meal. Now whether Banana was named Banana because of these bananas or whether bananas were so called because of Banana he could not discern. His doubt increased when, later on, he visited another village called Banana – where the bananas were tiny.

Often the villages were in pairs. One was fairly modern with rectangular huts containing wooden and fresh-air windows. The other was Pygmy and more traditional; its huts were small hemispheres made of just branches and leaves. Exceptions, of course, existed and were ever more plentiful. In one Pygmy settlement he heard some of the best music of the entire trip – only drums were used but all were played hard and fast, their rythms most subtely combined. In another such village, while he rested over a breakfast of avocados, some of the people came to look at and chat with him, or perhaps to trade; one tried to sell a complete adult crocodile skin for the equivalent of £2. Another was a young woman who wore, apart from the nini[11] (a splendid Swahili word which means sometimes what, sometimes the what-you-may-call-it, usually anything; it is especially used when one has forgotten the correct technical, polite or sophisticated word) over her loins, just one other 'garment'. It looked like a small pencil stub pushed into the upper lip. It was, he learnt, to enhance her beauty though Baha, distracted somewhat by the bare bosom, failed to comprehend its prominence.

Between these little pockets of humanity, where a few plants were nursed, stretched miles and miles of forest. Its density varied constantly as a multitude of greens were forever mixed in different combinations. It formed a perfect home for monkeys, lizards and similar little fellows. Birds were everywhere and insects too abounded, especially near the numerous rivers, all tributaries of the Zaire.

That night, as it was Christmas Eve, he went to a midnight service. The church, of reinforced mud construction, contained old tree trunks called wooden seats. Hymns, sung to the accompaniment of vibrating drums, were of course in Swahili except for those four words "Gloria in excelsis Deo". Outside, by day, here and in many towns, there was more music; drums were again beaten, songs were sung and swinging hips were lovely. Alas, it was not traditional; rather, all was political praising party and president and only sometimes a lover or a God.

Christmas lunch was breakfast, and both were a plate of rice. He ventured south; the day for most was not that different from others, there being few presents to give and no Queens to speak. Seasonal greetings however were many, be they 'bon fête' or 'siku kuu'. Numerous too were the road's corrugations and the wee forested hills over which the road ran but Baha pushed. Christmas was exhausting. He hoped to be able to finish the day in style, perhaps even with a beer, but just a few miles short of a town where limited celebrations might have been possible, both tyres, the sun and his hopes went down. The day finished over a piece of sugar cane, price 1½ pence, in a disused hut which leaked somewhat. A torchlight search of the roof revealed, apart from those leaky holes, rather ugly spiders. He switched off and tried to forget the presence of such creatures. At such a late hour, there was nowhere else to sleep. He returned to darkness and thought of home. Happy Christmas.

Towards the end of Boxing Day, the back wheel finally decided it had had enough. It buckled and rubbed continually against the frame. He tried to push on regardless but, although he pushed more and cycled less, he could not prevent the wheel from its final collapse. It died, cracked completely in one place and severely weakened in four others. Thus for the last hundred and twenty-five miles (200 kms) of forest before Kisangani, he had to get a lift. Here he unsuccessfully sought a new wheel while waiting for the boat to Kinshasa. This he had intended to take anyway as there was no direct road between the two towns: the river was the highway.

Food in the market was very varied; fruit and veg were plentiful; meat and fish were much sought after, by humans, dogs

30

and flies, the more so as dissections were performed on the spot; and small buns, similar to maandazi[12], made from peanuts and cooked in palm oil, bridged many of Baha's imaginary gaps. Thus he spent the New Year in comparative comfort though the mosquitoes possessed little festive unselfishmess. He invested in something cheap – a few square feet of mosquito net which barely covered his head.

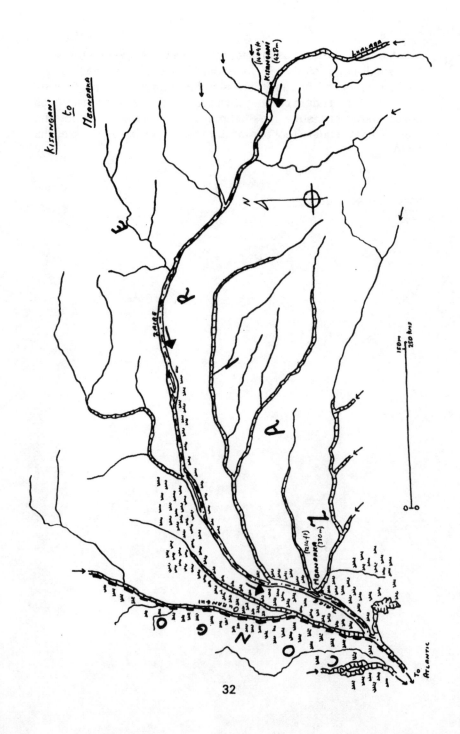

32

Chapter 3.

PEDAL OR PADDLE.

The seven day boat trip was a fascinating experience. While queueing for the ticket, he interrupted his novel to chat with a passer-by in French. When someone pushed from behind, he turned and asked brusquely, "Unafanya nini[11] (what are you doing)?" Others in the queue were indeed surprised – a mzungu[10] spoke in French, read in English and swore in Swahili! Yet most Africans speak two if not more languages. In Zaire, where there are four national languages besides the official one of French, this is invariably true; never did Baha find an African who could not speak his own tribal tongue.

He bought a second class ticket – wazungu[10] were not allowed to travel third or fourth class – and, after a day or two, climbed onboard. The boat consisted of one bit which contained the engine and the first class part, pushing a few second and third class barges and one enormous flat platform which was in front of everything. This was for anything and anybody else. Here were some stores as well as a few families and their belongings. Most of the passengers were going to Kinshasa where, if nothing else, they hoped to take advantage of the capital's inflated and urbanised prices.

At first, this large barge was not too full, and one was able to scramble up to the front, sit on a bollard and just watch Africa go by. On either side, the jungle was often dense; elsewhere one saw areas that were little more than bush. These occasionally bore signs of livelier days. Where once had stood those tall, straight trees whose only greenery was right at the top in one large ball of foliage, were now only their grey, dead trunks, stationary and silent. Death had come and only these skeletons remained. In the heart of the jungle some trees were always dying, making way for others soon to grow. It was not so here; death on such a large scale was probably the result of man's folly.

Every so often, one would see little villages clustered on the banks. Some of the houses were on stilts for fear of rising waters and wild animals like crocodiles or snakes. To their inmates, the river was a source of food and their only contact with the outside world. When the big boats came by (perhaps only a couple of times

33

a month), the locals would come to trade. Having sold their fish or meat to the passengers, they would be able to load up with clothes, tinned food, beer and cigarettes before the long paddle home, for by now, after all this bartering had been bargained for, the ship was a good few miles further downstream. Because of the high prices in Kinshasa, competition among the passengers for the villagers' foodstuffs was stiff.

Now the villagers came in their dug-out canoes or piroques[17] as they called them. These were anything up to fifteen yards long but only two feet (60 cms) wide. They rolled easily. Despite this, the fishermen always stood and used their long and sometimes beautifully carved oars as paddles or, in shallow waters, as punting poles. All worked in time, together. The river at sunset, when distant canoeists were silhouetted by a fading twilight, resembled a calm water upon which travelled in random directions so many silent and synchronised water beetles.

As a piroque[17] approached the ship, many prospective buyers scrambled up to the bow hoping to back a good buy. The fishermen, at this stage, were more worried about the immediate problem of bringing the piroque[17] in over the large wake and securing themselves before being swept swiftly astern for, unless the captain from his vantage point high up on the bridge had decided to buy the piroque's load himself, the ship would not have slowed down.

The fishermen, then, were rolling the piroque[17] in over the wake. The passengers jostled with each other hoping to see and book for themselves a good specimen. Reservation was done by throwing a rag onto the particular object. Some rags missed and were swept astern; others landed in the bilges and a few hit the fishermen themselves; but the rags kept a'coming in a mighty shower until all objects were claimed. By this time, the sailors were over the wake (not all were successful but fishermen swim and canoes float) and were moving rapidly astern before managing, while paddling like fury so as to ease the operation, to secure the prioque's bow firmly to the barge. Meanwhile the customers had been running over this obstacle course of a barge to where the canoe was so desperately trying to tie up. Then, there would follow the most incredible shauri[7] while men and women argued, in competition with the noise of the engine, not only about the price of each article but also whose rag it was, where it had landed, which one had landed first and, if not, why it hadn't but should have. It was a spectacle well worth witnessing . . . . once . . . . . at a distance . . . . from behind.

Gradually, the barge got more and more full, mainly of food; anything which moved, animal or child, was attached to something which didn't. There were fish, some alive and kept so in bowls, others (these included netted cat-fish, some six feet (1.8 m) long) freshly dead and stowed in large holds, and yet more smoked and stacked in baskets. Monkeys too were smoked – they looked horribly human for, apart from being cut down the middle and gutted, they were still complete; from a sitting position with arms and legs akimbo, their hollow eye sockets focused at infinity, and such emptiness was death. Others were definitely alive, playing happily on the end of a string. Baha was a little displeased when one such little fellow started pulling the hairs of Baha's legs. When it had found they were real, its mind was obviously coming to incorrect conclusions on the subject of monkeys' evolution. In similar fashion, little children, anywhere in the world, look at curious strangers. In Africa, too, if they had sufficient courage, they would test the hairs on a white man's legs for such growth was, to them, unusual. If one dislikes being the centre of active investigation, one should perhaps not travel alone. And in contrast, little Indian watoto[3] are intrigued by the way a European's skin is pink yet, when pressed, goes white before slowly returning to its natural pink.

To return to the barge. Onboard, cocks and chickens were put in wicker baskets hanging over the side so that droppings dropped unnoticed, except by an innocent leaning over a lower-deck guardrail; it was a shade odd to be afloat and yet woken in the mornings by cock crow. Pigeons and canaries completed the aviary section while elsewhere pigs and goats were noisily alive. Insects were represented by large and ugly slugs – there were large bowls of these brutes; all wriggled over and under each other, struggling in vain to remain on top of the orgy. Each was about three inches (7.5 cms) long and of such ugliness that both ends looked as if they were rears. And all these non-human creatures on board were foodstuffs. Perhaps the world hasn't got a food shortage after all – just the problem of how to persuade Baha and others to eat, among other things, these reversible slugs.

The front barge was by now a veritable village. Whole families were living there and something was always happening. Babies and clothes were being washed, fish watered, animals fed and meals cooked. By night, life was quieter as all curled on top of each other for a spot of sleep though animals failed to observe the peace. By day, noise came from one overworked record player, two and a half records and a no-fi loudspeaker at such a volume that everybody on this large collection of barges could hear and nobody could not. Slowly, the days passed. The captain would stop the ship in some of the larger villages and towns, or if rain obscured visibility too much — this could easily happen at night when searchlights were used. The scheduled stops were often delayed by visiting dignatories, a large number of whom appeared to roam the vast nation amidst much pomp! To greet them were inevitably an armed guard of motley recruits, a brass band of unrivalled or state-monopolised ability, and a bevy of wenches on a more dainty yet less equal footing. Nearby crowds would usually, should definitely, be happy. A plinth to the one and only party, the country, its independence and its President received the attention of all via lengthy speeches, songs and dances. A travelling visitor needed patience.

Navigation by arrows stuck on trees was novel, and far from easy in a river so enormous that it was sometimes ten miles (16 km) wide; stationary islands, some small, some up to fifty miles (80 km) long, and large drifting hunks of green vegetation did not help. Tributaries big enough to drown the Thames joined unnoticed. Landmarks sometimes did not exist. The river flowed through a flat swampy area and river banks were lost. Later, the river moved from the jungle to a hillier area where it narrowed and the current increased. Navigation returned to more commonly accepted methods. Though the scenery was constantly changing, the diet remained the same – rice twice a day. He was tolerably pleased to get to Kinshasa.

Now during his stay in the capital, he had three problems. The first one, how to look after himself, was most adequately solved by a family who had made the mistake of knowing Baha's rather more sensible brother. The second one was to repair the bike; alas, spares for his particular breed of vehicle were not to be found. Something just had to be done. In the end, he bought a 28-inch wheel as opposed to the original 26; it fitted, just. With this, a tyre and a tube or two, he went off while planning, if trials were successful, to return for some spare spokes.

And then there was the rather large third problem. His original visa was valid for a month – he now had just a few days left. As a European, he was not allowed to cross into Congo Brazzaville or Cabinda*. He had two alternatives; one was to get to Gabon, for which he had the necessary bumph, by some means or other. To fly was too expensive. To go by sea was, in theory at least, possible. The other thought was to extend the visa and head for Zambia. This he tried; but he ran into difficulties. He had to prove that he had been spending the equivalent of twenty U.S. dollars a day and that he had sufficient funds to continue such extravagance. (He knew and had known about this rule, and it was the only one he had deliberately not even attempted to obey – for obvious reasons. In any case, to do so on a bicycle in the bush is none too easy). Furthermore, a month's extension took about three weeks to be cleared, by which time, of course, one would have to start applying for another. He could, as another plan, have tried going south to Angola but this would have required special permission and in any case few immigration officials north of the Zambezi liked chaps with Portugese stamps in their passports. So only one answer remained – to go to Gabon by sea. Most big ships went straight to Europe; he would have to find a fisherman.

Because of the twenty dollar rule, he realised it would be better to leave the country at a nice, quiet, little and therefore perhaps also unmeticulous border post. Thus he decided to nip down to the coast, to the little fishing village of Banana, and there try for a boat. A glance at the map showed that the verb 'to nip down' applied to a distance greater than that from London to Blackpool. There was no time to lose.

The next morning, without even going back to buy those spare spokes, he set off, hoping. If this plan didn't work, he would be stuck and, after a day or two or being thus stuck, he would be illegally so. Life was a bit worrying, but the wheel seemed to be working well and, in open and hilly country, life was tranquil. Hunger soon

---

* At this time, the Portugese colonies of Angola and Mozambique had not received independence, nor in fact had the April '74 Portugese coup, which made possible such independence, taken place. Cabinda, as an enclave of Angola, was therefore in Portugese hands and not liked by Zaire. Also, relations between Congo Brazzaville and Zaire had for some time been tense; relaxations were beginning but some border restrictions were still in force.

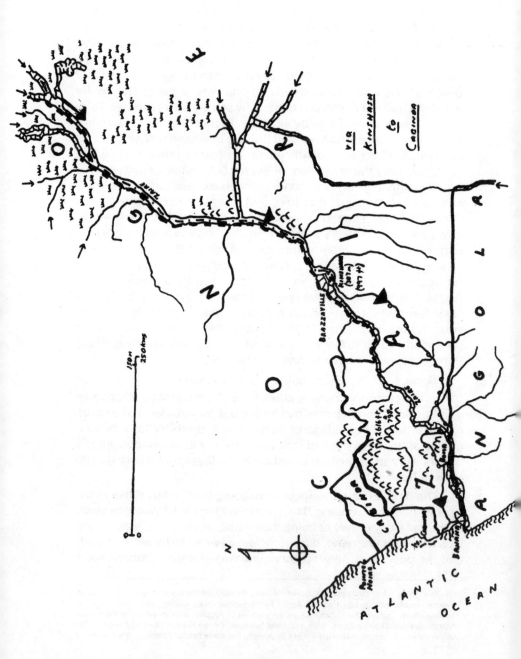

returned. In one small village he went to see what was for sale in the one and only tiny dukah[4]. He found just one item – a bowl of live caterpillars. Hunger immediately faded, but not for long. In another village, a bigger dukah[4] was found. He was invited into the sitting room, sat down and served with a helping of bread and fish in splendid style. Afterwards payment was refused. He was most impressed with this generosity. He later learnt that some of the Zairois in Kinshasa had referred to him as "Le pauvre (the poor man)" – if a mzungu[10] had only got a bicycle, he must be poor! Later, a lorry overtook him and offered him a lift. He declined at first but, having gone through a village where the lorry had stopped, he was overtaken again, shown an approaching rain cloud and persuaded. Because of his expiring visa, this lift was invaluable. At midnight on the Saturday, he arrived in Boma where he shared a fire, the night and some mosquitoes with the askari[13] or nightwatchman at the local church.

In the morning, after praying quite hard, for it looked as if some assistance would be necessary, he set off for Banana. It was a flat, sandy and lonely road though at one or two roadblocks, policemen questioned his nationality and motives. The area was a little sensitive. Food here was a problem – apart from the odd bit of fruit, there was little to eat except bread and fish. In villages there was nothing else. In towns, variety was too expensive. His lunch was substantiated with a beer which, near Kinshasa, is the cheapest liquid on sale.

Later, on a tiresome, sandy stretch of road, he stopped. It was just too 'damn' hot. The air was still and, at slow speeds, inevitable in such conditions, there was no cooling, relative wind. He rested under a tree and waited for a cloud to cover the sun. And so, shortly afterwards, he was pushing again for wet sand is no good for bicycles. African weather, like those country buses which can be either very fast or stationary, was sometimes able to contemplate only two alternatives: a boiling sun or a drenching rain. A nice, cooling, moderate British drizzle, or pleasant motoring, were seldom considered. It was a short storm, and he reached the coast safely, leaving him with just two days to solve problems and exit the country.

On his first visit to the beach he met, on a wide expanse of sand, only two people: one bartender and one fisherman. The former thought the idea of sailing a piroque[17] to Gabon was crazy;

39

the latter said it was good, conned a beer out of him, and then disappeared. So Baha then toured other parts of the coastline. There really was very little. The local fishermen all used piroques[17] and rarely went more than one hundred yards offshore. Here they would drop their nets before pulling them back unto the beach. Grimsby trawlers just had not been invented. And nobody wanted to either paddle to Gabon or commit suicide – extraordinary.

There was only one answer. He would have to buy a piroque[17] and go alone. He remembered from his earlier sailing days, (as a lad, Baha had spent some years 'before the mast'), that there was a northbound current in this part of the Atlantic. He went for a swim and tested it. He swam again after the tide had changed and it was still there. Good. He went to buy the piroque[17]. First prices were the equivalents of £35 to £50 which, for just a dug-out canoe, were a shade inflationery. He eventually got one for £20 – he was still 'done' but it was, on that particular day only, a seller's market.

That night he slept, a little illegally for one of those twenty dollar reasons, on the beach in order to study the weather and confirm local fishermen's reports. The research, however, turned out to be more zoological rather than meteorological. He was plagued by crabs, white jobs some four or five inches (10-12 cms) across or head on, as it were. They kept on coming up the beach for a night feed. They didn't like barricades or torchlight, but Baha's efforts at keeping them at bay by the use of such were unsuccessful. He tried many times to sleep, but these chaps scrambling over his limbs were a bit much. As the night wore on, tiredness ensured sleep. Now normally he was a heavy sleeper but there were limits. One crab woke him up by walking across his face! They were everywhere. A thousand curses. Not he, nor them, only the ocean was calm. This, if nothing else, was good news. The sea seemed to be tolerably peaceful except for a short time after lunch. What lunch? Every meal these days continued to be one loaf of bread and a tin of fish. For the time being, Baha was enjoying no miracles.

In the morning, he thought it wise to stock up with food and clear immigration (he had to prove that he had bought the canoe and that he wasn't leaving just to go to Angola or Cabinda; happily he got no twenty dollar questions), before carrying out some surf riding trials. The piroque[17] had first to be carried a couple of hundred yards to the water. It was placed on two small cross bars and these in turn were placed on four heads, one of which was

Baha's soft cranium. It must have weighed a ton and more. That part of the journey was most uncomfortable. From its lofty height, it bounced, banged and bruised. His poor, unaccustomed nut received hurts from above and odd looks from the side. The few locals who were by the roadside had not often seen a mzungu[10] carry something on his head.

Once on the beach, the three helpers stood by as Baha launched himself into the Atlantic surf. Disaster struck; both capsized. His second attempt ended in a similar humiliation. He decided not to inform them of his earlier maritime career. He did, however, give up the trial. An assisted launch showed that paddling in the deep water beyond the surf was definitely feasible and fairly safe. He would just have to accept the fact that once launched, he would have to stay at sea until the journey's end – where ever that would be. The bicycle and gear were now loaded on and in the canoe. All spare tubes were inflated and tied down – "mustn't waste this chance of extra bouyancy", he thought. Then there were just two things left to do, possibly for the last time; he first went into the nearby village church, and then he had a beer. The barman still thought he was crazy.

He realised that what he was doing was dangerous. The canoe would only remain dry in anything less than a force two. And the Atlantic, especially by night, is lonely and not a little large. He might be swept out to sea, or perhaps the canoe would fill with water. Either way, a death due to starvation, thirst, exposure or fish was possible. Somehow, a sort of faith in a God gave him hope.

By four o'clock, the wind was beginning to die down. It was time to go. With considerable assistance, the loaded canoe was brought to the water. Then, into the water, all pushing. In the excited surf, there were cries of "Montez, montez (climb in, climb in)". Baha thought they were being unnecessarily British, patriotic and sentimental, before remembering that they were talking French. He jumped aboard and started paddling. A mighty shove from behind ensured his successful passage through the breakers. He was at sea, and only a little bit of it was inside the canoe.

The paddle was a useless, heavy device with but one blade – alas, there had been nothing else. Progress was slow, though the current was true. And the sunset was delightful; a great ball of red illuminated the steep coast in ever deepening hues. The wind, as scheduled, was dying, and the smooth waters reflected all. At one stage, he had to paddle further out to sea for a bit of rough water indicating a shallow patch of rocks and, no doubt, packets of detergent. All was soon well again. The paddle was rested for a supper of bread, unfortunately soaked somewhat by that surf, and tomatoes. Salt sir? Africa drifted slowly by. Quiet .... peace .... bliss. "What more could a man ask for", he thought, "apart perhaps from a wife who would prevent one from having such distorted ideas of happiness. Still", he continued, "it was nice to know, despite all those usual signs of age creeping on, that one was still young enough to be stupid". At a bell-less eight o'clock or thereabouts, he left Zaire's national and maritime boundaries. He was legal with four hours to spare.

In the morning, in order to remain inside the law, he would have to be outside Cabinda's territorial waters. These he assumed to be three miles. Icelandic alternatives would have been somewhat prohibitive. For the time being, however, all was quiet and it didn't really matter. He moved a bit further out for another shallow patch but then, with the Atlantic a dead flat calm like a sleeping giant, he had little to worry about. His mother, he later learnt, never reached the same degree of confidence but she, after all, was only able to worry retrospectively. He alternately paddled and slept, using his rucksack as a backrest-cum-pillow, and knowing full well that an incoming ocean would act as a very good alarm clock. Occasionally he ate some fruit and some more damp bread – he had about four days' provisions on board. His one worry was lavatorial; because of the canoe's instability he dared not move higher than a sitting position. A capsize, even though the canoe would not have sunk below the surface, would have been the end. He was able to have a pee by lying down, arching his back and aiming far. But to his future lavatorial needs, no solution offered itself.

"Well", he thought, "I could bare the bottom, and from a lying position protrude the posteria o'er the leeward gunwhale. But such exposure to the elements might involve a browner base than usual, even in circumstances of such a salty flush. And then, of course, the elements might include the dreadful shark, which could nip me in the bud . . . bum . . . . budum". These thoughts were not conducive to nautical soirees, normally associated with calm evenings, guardails, tropical seas, silver moons and underarm deodorants. "There again, a shark contemplating a quick nosh might be put off if it paused to think – or smell. Thereagainagain, if it likes the best bit at the end, I suppose it must start with the bad bits, even if the worst bit is the end".

A second alternative was essential. "Well perhaps I'll just have to lie down, stick my stomach up into the air, and hope that such a concave excretion won't be too messy". Again, complications disturbed his calm. Perhaps, while arms were busily engaged in holding up the back, a simultaneous uncontrolled pee might cause an unnecessary and hardly cleansing fountain. And in any case, his muscles might not be able to maintain the arch for sufficient time; a collapse would see him end up end down in the . . . . er . . . . oh.

A third arrangement was hunted for, but in vain. What to do? Something, down there, was happening. Oh heavens, was this it? But no – he passed wind; such miniscule protest was soon lost amidst the enormous Atlantic sky. He returned his musings to the other end, and ate another bit of soggy bread.

Navigation, at this stage, was fairly easy. On leaving Zairois waters, he could see a glow in the sky which he assumed was the town of Cabinda. He expected to see another glow later and this would indicate the other large town some thirty miles (48 kms) further north. Sure enough, as time progressed, a second glow appeared as expected. He navigated accordingly, keeping the glows to starboard. He knew the coast at Cabinda was slightly concave and thus he calculated he would be about four miles off the coast by daybreak. Then, however, life became confusing. What was one and then two glows became three, four and more. The moon arriving at midnight failed to clarify the situation. Time showed that these orange glows were flares and, just before dawn, well over twenty of them were visible. First light saw Baha near a large off-shore oilfield! Those 'shore' lights had been at sea; all were simple structures burning off the excess gas found on top of oil pockets in previous drillings. No-one had told him about this, least of all his 1:4000000 map! As a result, he was about seven miles off shore and that, for a dug-out canoe, was a little excessive he thought. A breeze blowing him partially westwards and partially backwards did not help, especially psychologically. However, where there is oil there should be life and there it was: among all those flares he could just make out the three legs of an oil rig. Because these glows had been from oil and not the town of Cabinda, he now didn't really know where he was. And because he was so far out at sea, he could not tell whether or not the current was still helping him. These questions required answers before night returned. There too was the distant silhouette of an ancient-looking Portugese frigate, slowly heading back to port – ummm . . . .

Legally speaking, he thought, the oil rig was on the high seas, and in any case, he knew that international maritime law allowed sailors in distress to seek shelter in coastal waters regardless of nationality. It took a very small wave to convince Baha of his distress. More than sufficient proof appeared imminent as a great rain cloud approached from the North West. Rain is often associated with and announced by wind and therefore waves. This immediate problem occupied Baha for the next hour or so. He kept the waves fine on his port bow, though such a noun was a little too inappropriate for such a blunt and assymetrical hunk of a trunk. Paddling was often curtailed because of bailing operations – many a little wave was breaking in over the gunwhale. In the rain, visibility was considerably reduced and all signs of life were obscured. Again, he was alone.

As the rain cleared he caught sight of the oil rig once more. It was a bit nearer, as indeed it should have been, but it looked as if he had been swept even further out to the West, despite the wind

44

pushing him to the South East. Baha, during his sojourn with the Ugandan police, had read about the Kon-Tiki expedition, and he knew a similar westward current existed in the southern Atlantic. The imagination began to work overtime with thoughts of drifting into the westward blue. A trans-Atlantic transportation of a bicycle by canoe would, on consideration, be of little anthropological value. To reach that oil rig, even if only to ask a few questions, became the all-important task, especially as more rain clouds were approaching. Because of these, the prospects of an afternoon on-shore breeze were negligible. Paddling was hard work and

progress was slow. The rig was bigger and further away than he had thought. By measuring with his little finger the angle subtended by the drilling platform, he knew he was gradually getting closer. That was comfort.

At about two o'clock, he arrived. He struggled with paddle and bailer to keep himself in position in the turbulent waters underneath the rig while many faces, many feet up, looked down. This, a fish's eye view of an oil rig, made it look enormous. Three bulbuous, middle-aged legs rose to support a large platform on which cranes, derricks, winches, drills, generators and helicopters all hummed actively. Yet, within the parameters of the Atlantic, it was as it had been when first sighted with the dawn – tiny. For some minutes, which seemed interminable, only mutual admiration took place for the wind made communication at this distance impossible. Soon however, a chap was lowered in a basket. He looked at Baha, asked a few questions and then ascended once more. The struggle with wind and wave continued, but not for long. A scrambling net was lowered. He tied the piroque[17] to this as best he could and then climbed up. This he found incredibly difficult – indeed at the top he could barely stand atill. He wobbled, while his eyes wandered even more drunkenly at his new surroundings – he had always wanted to visit an oil rig!

His reception was a little mixed. Some Americans who appeared to be in charge, merely demanded his passport and called him a damned idiot. An Englishman said that he was jolly lucky to be alive for apparently there were many dangerous currents around these areas about which he, being retired navy actually old boy, knew so much. Again Baha decided to remain silent about his own naval past. Many Africans just looked at him with horror-cum-curiosity: yet another stupid mzungu[10] (a word derived from the verb kuzungu – to wander). But he received more than solace from an Irishman who, when told of a mid-Atlantic canoeist with a bicycle, had told his informer to eff off. Paddy led Baha away from the air-conditioned yanks to the canteen where everything edible and eatable was for the taking.

"Well I've always wanted to do something different too", he said, but Baha's mouth was full. Not only was it the first time he had seen an oil rig – here was a real ice-cream machine. He was soon stable. Then the officials returned to inform him of the presence of the Portugese Navy. He was being arrested – again. This he felt was against maritime law; but he also decided that a chap in a canoe has little to offer against the diplomacy of a gun-boat, albeit pre-war, and that a prison is probably safer than a piroque[17]. He climbed down that dreadful net again to find that his boat was hanging on by only the front wheel (an unusual maritime situation). The lashings were not holding up to the buffetings of these troubled seas. Half an hour later would probably have seen a bicycle suspended and submerged on the end of the rope, a waterlogged piroque[17] drifting down wind, and a 'rucksacksunk'. His sojourn at sea was at an end, but he had received at least one blessing: twenty four hours of sitting in salt water had caused the boils on both buttocks to completely disappear.

Soon he was in a police station. Around him were several policemen all heavily disguised as plain clothes civilians, jumping up and down, waving all limbs frantically, demanding instant answers to their numerous questions most of which were in French, none in English. In the middle stood Baha, jumping up and down, frantically waving not only limbs, trying to find out where the loo was. Yet again, he had got diarrhoea. Indeed, because of the 'salted' bread, the yanks' air conditioned offices which had caused a rain soaked Baha to shiver noticeably, and the ice-cream machine, he was definitely ill. Questioning was interrupted several times by rushed visits to the bog. And the visits to the bog were also interrupted by further questions – now that was definitely not British. How can one possibly retain the stiff upper lip when one's trousers are down? Keep up what flag? He later learnt that the Portugese authorities suspected that he, in canoe with bike, was an Arab terrorist or an Angolan freedom fighter who had come to blow up oil installations but who, having failed, was trying to flush away secret documents.

He was kept in the prison for five days while his motives were checked. Time for another chapter of the memoirs. His only discomfort were the large cockroaches which shared his cell, but at least by day he was allowed to walk around the yard. Communication was difficult for neither side really knew much French. The climax was reached when the chief policeman lost his temper because of Baha's persistence and in exasperation shouted at the top of his voice, "Très calme, très calme (patience, patience)!" Baha's 'sang froid' ensured the chief got stuck in this noisy groove for some long seconds. Cross references to the recently celebrated six hundred years of Anglo-Portugese friendship didn't help.

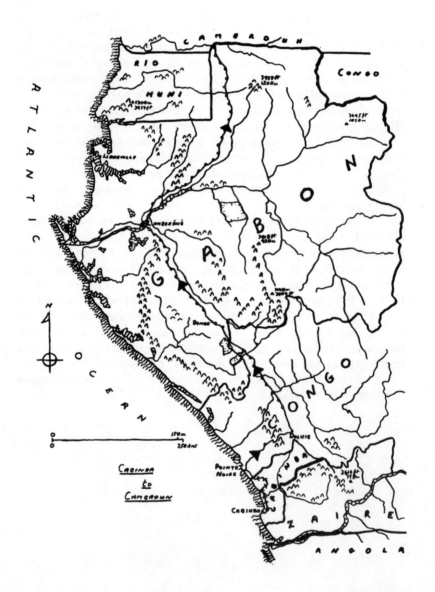

CAMEROUN

CONGO

RIO

MUNI

ATLANTIC

GABON

ONGO

OCEAN

N

0   150m
0   250kms

Cabinda
to
Cameroun

POINTE
NOIRE

CABINDA

ZAIRE

ANGOLA

48

Chapter 4.

PUSHED FOR TIME.

After five days he was reunited with his still somewhat salty bike and driven north to the Congo-Brazzaville border. Here, he and it were deposited with a large, Latin sigh of relief. His canoe was never seen again. He didn't mind. He couldn't.

Baha climbed on and off he went. An ominous rubbing noise came from his back wheel. The sea had done it no good. Rust was surface but widespread. Many noises normally associated with unemployed violinists emanated from several parts, but his first concern was to get a Congolese stamp in his passport for, in theory, he was an illegal visitor. The Portugese authorities had ordered him to tell the Congolese officials a pack of lies about his occupation – somewhat odd behaviour for policemen – but this Baha felt would be rather stupid and might even be asking for another arrest! As it happened, he was welcomed, given a little stamp and told to see more officials in Pointe-Noire for a bigger one. Only then would he be a legal tourist. He rode off – or rather, he tried. That oversized rear wheel was now bent. He removed the brakes; progress was then possible. He made a few attempts at stopping by rubbing his shoes against the back wheel but these were not really very successful. He resolved to proceed gently and to sort out the mechanics after Pointe-Noire.

A mile or two later saw, by a small bridge, a happy group of villagers – or so he thought. They waved and shouted, both in French, with enthusiasm. They appeared to be very friendly, but Baha wanted this big stamp more than just a chat. He cycled on. Within a couple of hundred yards, he was suddenly overtaken and waved to a stop by a car full of chaps in uniform. No brakes! Absentmindedly, his hands grabbed the brakes although nothing was at the other end. He was slowing, but not quickly enough. He swerved to avoid hitting the car and, while the cops were getting out, jumped off and pulled it to a halt, smiling broadly as if he always did it this way.

And thus he learnt two things. Those villagers had not all been waving happily. And secondly, it is not good for bikes, shoes or personal decorum, to stop without brakes. A spoke or two had been broken and his rear brake holders were now bent. Another lesson. He repaired his front brakes before advancing further.

At Pointe-Noire, he was received most cordially and granted six days in which to get to Gabon. He also received some advice concerning the road to Dolisie: 'go by train'. This, like all good advice, he ignored. And that evening, climbing out of the town on a good road heading east across open grass lands while the sun was sinking into that old Atlantic behind him, he felt he had made the right decision. He was offered rest and a maize cob in a little village which had hidden itself among the palms. Later, lying on a bamboo bed and thankful that all bureaucracies had allowed him perhaps reluctantly to continue, he contemplated sleep. He was disturbed however by what he thought were mosquitoes on his shoulder. From a position high above his head, he brought his arm down with a mighty force which hopefully would bring death to the beasts. SPLASH! Splash? It should have been splat. He was not, afterall, plagued by insects – just sweating profusely.

The next day proved conclusively that that earlier advice had been correct. The road deteriorated quickly. The open grass lands changed to dense forest. Knowing he was only allowed to have a few days in Congo-Brazzaville and also that his Cameroun visa was to become invalid shortly, he determined to take what lifts he could. Progress otherwise on this often wet and muddy road was indeed slow. Three lifts helped him over the same number of miles. Roundabout noon, he stopped in a little village which stood at the edge of the forest proper, and there he bought some bananas called lunch. Thinking of lifts, he asked of the possibilities of cars along this road:

"Jamais (never)" was the sole answer.

"Jamais?"

"Jamais".

Still working on that good cyclists' principle of never going backwards, he continued. The last building in the village was the local school. It was typical of many in these countries, consisting of but one room wherein everyone was taught all levels of their primary education. Visual aids sometimes included a blackboard. A single teacher might have up to fifty kids in his care. The building, because of the heat, was open; (examinations during rainy seasons are not always easy). As Baha was riding by, he tried not to cause a distraction. Such, however, was the friendliness that the schoolmaster was the first to wave. The kids joined in enthusiastically; ah, few discipline problems exist when the teacher wants to play as well.

Riding was possible where the road permitted, though the back wheel was getting no better. Punctures ensured further variety. With one, he had just turned the bicycle upside down and was preparing to undo the wheel when there, through the spokes, he saw an enormous spider. Thinks. Later, he came to another small

village. On the way in, a boy joined in conversation with him and it appeared he was going to give Baha shelter for the night. Dad, however, had different ideas, but only because his house was really too small for any visitors. So Baha bid farewell, went to the market to stock up with food and then headed out into the forest again. Chaps in the village had been a bit noisy – this part of the world doesn't see many wazungu[10], certainly not on bicycles; indeed, one village earlier had downed everything and given him a standing ovation. Hoping for peace and quiet, he thought he would seek shelter in the village's suburbs. Often there were isolated little homes within spitting distance of a larger community. But not always. Baha had made another mistake. He was soon in the open forest; the sun was rapidly going down and he was slowly getting further and further away from human life. He continued, still hoping to find someone ahead, still not wishing to go backwards. The inevitable happened. He was alone in the jungle and it was dark.

Interesting. He found a large bamboo tree, under which was a lot of dead shrubbery which made a not-too-uncomfortable bed. The tree was large enough to hide himself and the bicycle though from whom or what was never determined. He washed in the adjacent river, ate a pineapple and then, before falling off to sleep on top of his sleeping bag – it was quite hot – he remembered that vast, dual-tone spider. Er . . . . he put his long trousers on.

Happily, on waking, both bicycle and trousers were where he had left them.

He had suspected, the previous evening, that there had been a home 'just around the corner'. His suspicions had been unfounded however, though there were many corners as the road wound its way up the valley. Occasionally it passed that railway line; here he was tempted away from what was little more than a farm track. It would have been straighter and less hilly certainly, but pushing a bike over sleepers would tire any man's patience. He stuck to the road, often literally. Uphill he pushed because it was steep; downhill because of the stones; and nohill because of the mud.

Most of the time he was alone. There were one or two settlements, the first indications of which were little graves, mounds of earth under tiny corrugated iron roofs, which lay by the roadside. To Baha, these graves meant villages, people and therefore food – they were a sign of life. In the forest there was indeed little, just the odd villager or rarer party cadre in a Che Guevara hat. There were occasional little groups of huts, rectangular wicker constructions usually on stilts. The men, of course, sat and chatted and watched. Their women carried many wares in long canoe-shaped baskets on top of their heads.

The hills were many and getting bigger. He was climbing. The rivers were thinning into streams, all of which offered superb views as they noisily bounced along over well-washed stones while playing with the numerous beams of bright sunlight which the trees allowed through. He was now pushing uphill the whole time while the road curved from one shoulder to another in its attempt to surmount this mountain range. As always on climbing, the obstacle got bigger as one got nearer: each rise revealed another previously hidden, each hairpin led to another valley, around which a second one would weave. Gaps in between the trees – some of these were up to one hundred feet (30 m) high – gave superb views over to the hilly west where the sun was starting to turn red. He was alone, humanly speaking, but after the previous night he felt confident about another bamboo'd bed.

There were enough other creatures around though. The main noise came from insects; one whole area would make a grasshopper-type sound and then go quiet while another area responded. This process was repeated with more and more volume as the dusk approached. Birds were everywhere, eating some of the insects and adding to the general cacophany, while monkeys preferred solo parts. The overall noise levels were quite fantastic – noise abatement groups should not only think of airports. Indeed, in this forest, everybody who so wished could complain, some hopefully might even get lost.

Baha watched a beautiful sunset over miles and miles of rolling jungle before climbing over the top to find a spot from which he would be able to see a good sunrise. He took some time to find, in this vast forest, a suitable bed. To discover a good bamboo among so many, such varied, such thick vegetation was not so easy. Darkness forced him to compromise. He tied everything together as a deterrent against souvenir-collecting monkeys. He spilt a load of antiseptic on a leg wound which thorns had re-opened – it was beginning to throb a little, giving him ample excuse for a wee bit of self pity. And in the still of the evening, insects buzzed, birds sang, monkeys squeaked, nothing bit, Baha slept.

Bamboos for comfort are now highly recommended, for he slept right through the sunrise. Later, the morning was pleasant indeed and it was all downhill. He was accompanied by streams which, a reflection of the previous day's climb, now swelled into rivers. Soon, he was out of the forest; he could ride .... (music please). And he could speak again, for here were people, going about their daily business. Then there was Dolisie, where chaps sped on mopeds. Baha ate, shaved off a healthy stubble and covered his fixed ratio gear in a dollop of grease before riding off again. A quick calculation suggested that if he was going to get to

Gabon in the time allowed, he would have to break a world record.

To the west was that mountainous forest which he now admired and respected. Here, he was on the flat amid green, rolling plains. The miles ticked by, and reasonably quickly. He was on the main road, a laterite one, a pleasant improvement. Then . . . . bang!

"What was that?" thought Baha, "the world record?" Alas no; it was the ratchet nini[11] on his rear wheel which had resigned. The end was at foot. Riding was now impossible, and soon he was in a lorry. Some of the scenery here was most odd; it would appear that at this juncture, the creator had got somewhat bored of world making and had decided to amuse himself. On what was otherwise a flat plain were scattered numerous green, up,turned, near-perfect semi-spheres for, to Baha's low level of mortal intellect, no apparent reason. It looked rather like the closing scene of a large and largely unsuccessful cookery lesson. The vegetation was mainly grass, some three or four feet (about 1m) tall, but occasionally there were small gatherings of trees usually situated on the banks of the many streams of beautifully clear water which were for ever coming out of the forest. Of people, villages and so on, there were very few signs.

He moved from lift to lift. Once, his pushing was noticed and two locals offered assistance. Baha stood helpless while this ratchet device was taken off and to bits. He had never seen the insides of one before. The fault was discovered, an old sardine tin was sacrificed and with two small bits thereof, the nini[11] was reassembled. After a lunch of boiled manioc or cassava (not so good), and boiled peanuts, (they were better), he recommenced riding. The back wheel was still twisted, its spokes were getting fewer, but at least it was going round, albeit noisily. And thus he crossed the border, in time.

In the next village, he sat on the grass verge for what he hoped would be forty winks. Peace was cancelled, however, for from behind, many a kid burst forth from a school to look at this odd visitor. Questions followed, some of which were Baha's concerning their textbooks; one was for new maths, while a second concerned, under the slightly ambiguous heading of social studies, their glorious president, mighty without precedent.

Punctures were a little bit more troublesome at this time, for Baha was not accustomed to these French wheels. The tyres were much bigger in all respects than the wheel for which they were nevertheless intended. To get the tyre to sit properly on the wheel was difficult; rather like, he thought, putting an over-sized bra onto an under-sized bosom. He thought indeed. The final puncture of the day was a major one: along with the air went another spoke and the tyre! This last had apparently had enough of all that rubbing against the frame. So, yet again, Baha was in a helpless situation. Many chaps offered assistance but all he could do was accept a lift into Dendé where he spent the night. In consolation, he drank rather a nice cup of tea made from a plant which resembled grass.

The bike was definitely ill. Being without spokes and unable to buy any spares meant much walking. That Cameroun visa was still worrying and it looked as if Yaoundé would be the first town big enough to supply the necessary spare parts. Walking was hot work. When cycling, one usually had a relative wind which cooled one, but walking was too slow. Only late in the day, when all his water had been drunk, did he get a short lift to a town. Here he was stopped by police who, instead of questioning and interrogating, gave him a beer – a welcome interpretation of the written word. And just before nightfall, after a woman had insisted on plying him with sugar cane, an old lorry came by. The bike was hurled on top of a load of plantains and off they went into the night and forest. At about one o'clock in the morning, the lorry stopped in a little village where an all night party of dancing was going on. Baha was offered a wooden bed for a few hours. At five, he was woken and off they drove again. The party was still under way. He was told that this traditional festivity was a birthday but he suspected the validity of the answer. In the next village, another party looked as if it too was just beginning.

At Lambaréné, while waiting for the ferry, he saw a cow being slaughtered. Charming. It seemed to accept death quite happily, while all its selfish mates just continued to chew the tropical cud. It was Sunday, and so off to church where he was offered a tap with which to wash himself and his clothes. He was glad he had his swimming trunks with him; many church-goers had not yet given prayer their undivided attention on account of this near naked, bathing mzungu[10]. Washing in public was not Baha's forte. Eventually, he also prayed, while his clothes offered up water vapour.

Time to start walking again. It was another hot day. In one little village he asked for water. An old man brought a cup. As a general rule, in the interests of hygiene, Baha liked to drink 'see-through' water. If he could see the bottom of the cup, it was probably pure enough. But on raising this one to his lips he paused, for there, in the water, was something moving. It was a small nini[11], about one inch (2.5 cms) long and definitely alive – fresh, one could have indeed said. As in all such instances, however, he felt bound to drink lest the old man be offended. It would probably have been better not to look at all. Cheers.

His next stop was for the night; it had been a long day's not so long walk. He was welcomed into a lonely homestead and introduced by Dad to all the family. First there were the three wives who seemed to be very happy sharing the one husband, looking after him and his needs, as it were, in watches. This involved team-work, and an ésprit de corps was definitely strong. They stood, smiling, arm in arm, like a victorious world-cup soccer squad. Secondly, there was grand-dad who, regretting his earlier monogamous existence, now contented himself with a pipe. And there were the kids. The first born considered his dad had definitely bettered his grandfather's performance, and he was determining in his eleven-year-old mind how he would do better than both. He was going to carve out a bit of the jungle for himself and there settle down with one wife. Later, as he conquered and cultivated more land (no planning permission needed) he, and she, would need another wife for there would be much work to be shared. To the amount of land conquered, or the number of wives married, there was no limit. What an incentive to work! The law of the jungle.

After a bath in a bucket, and a meal of 'banana bread' and spicy soups for dad, first-born and Baha only, there started a social evening, to which many a neighbour came. Wine, made from palms and sugar cane, was poured from enormous flagons. The servings were very liberal; the white, fluffy liquid only keeps for five days so consumption had to be considerable. The atmosphere was good. Towards the end of the long evening, all suddenly fell quiet when mum, the most senior wife, signalled that she wished to speak. Looking constantly at Baha, she spoke at length in her tribal tongue. He was unable to comprehend a word. He did, however, understand her arm movements: she drew the index finger of her right hand quickly in front of her throat while saying the word 'Fang'. It was obvious that all present considered her speech wise. Translations into French followed. Index fingers again moved across throats and

all repeated 'Fang'. This 'Fang' sounded rather English. Apparently, the 'Fang' tribe, who lived to the north, were regarded as blood-thirsty cut-throats! Baha had been thus warned. And so to bed.

He rose with the sun. Every other adult was already smoking a pipe, mainly because of numerous pestering little flies. Soon he was on the road and heading, via lifts and pushes, through Fang country. The only incident was more than unduly friendly. In what he thought was the last lift of the day were many locals travelling home after seeing their President visit the provincial town. His speech had included advice on being kind to tourists. Providentially, they thought, they met Baha. Before turning off, they all persuaded a local dukah[4] owner of this visitor's importance. Oh how British politicians would rejoice if they thought their constituents not only believed their every word, but immediately put them all into practice; (but what confusion would result). Before Baha knew what was happening, he was being led into the man's hut and offered the double bed – without wife of course. She had been given the mud floor. Baha's futile attempts at refusal were curtailed when

57

another lorry came by and took him through the night to the Cameroun border. He arrived half an hour before his visa, and therewith permission to enter the country, expired. And thus he came to Yaoundé, where he bought many a spare part for the bike. Soon he was ready to cycle again; his knowledge of bicycles was improving.

One further Gabonese incident was not forgotten: on one busy street, he saw an African couple bid each other good-bye. Gently, husband pecked at Madame's cheeks while her eyes only just condescended to such affection. It was a completely un-African gesture. To Baha's British mind, it was obviously French; no doubt a Frenchman in Kenya would be equally appalled by the obviously British mayoral robes, graduate gowns and justices' wigs. The next generation of Africans will probably not wish to tolerate such artificialities.

The African, as a rule, does not kiss his woman in public. He will, however, show friendliness, by holding hands, to his chum. Baha, on many occasions, had seen African policemen walking on duty hand in hand. It had taken some years before he was able to accept such behaviour as, at least not odd.

The country of Gabon, with its one or two 'Europe-orientated' industries, with its new-born development resulting in a broken down imported car in every village, with its ancient inertia still to bend rather than just be knocked, reminded one of a girl, a poor young and innocent girl who had lost her virginity before learning how to spell it.

It was good to be on the road again, cycling. It was not so good that the road, heading west from Yaoundé, was laterite. Often, at the bottom of some of the many hills, the road would suddenly be full of corrugations; there, a bicycle, the only road machine without suspension, was most unhappy, vibrating along like a fast and heavy centipedal robot. Tubes and spokes were often replaced, though Baha had thought life sufficiently varied by the changing

58

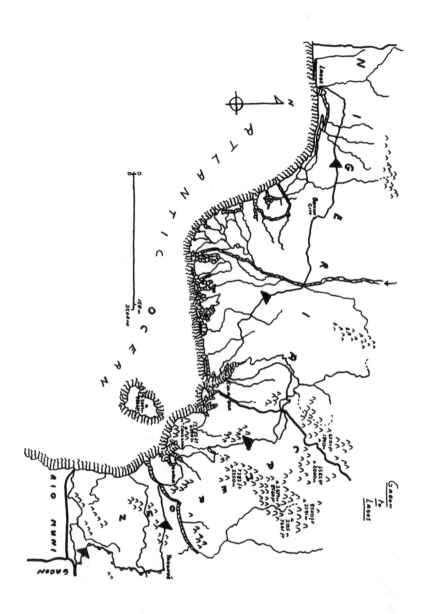

scenery in this hilly part of the rain forest. The trees were straight and tall, while others filled the lower gaps. Sunsets were obscured by the hamatan[14], the northerly wind that brings a dust of very fine sand from the Sahara at this time of the year. Visibility everywhere was reduced by this mist, and in the evenings, a large red ball of a sun would just gradually fade away. On the way to Douala, where the forest thinned to bush, he had another pleasant evening, sitting on the dry earth outside the headman's hut, drinking palm wine with some local village elders. The bottom was sore, but the belly was soon content.

And in Douala he proved, only to his own satisfaction, that he had mastered the French language to a tolerable degree. Proof of same must surely involve an argument and the successful completion thereof. He was overtaken in the city's heavy evening traffic – a majority of the road-users were on bicycles, many without lights, most without worries – by a fellow cyclist who collided with Baha's unilluminated tentpoles. He started off the argument with a French 'unafanya nini (what are you doing)?' and there followed few signs of British cool.

Later, on the open and tarmac road once more, he found his first dukah[4] since Zaire, though in Yaoundé bus station, little stalls had sold pretty well everything including monkeys' legs and antelopes. This new dukah[4] was in a little market. The meal was cassava served with a fish-cum-vegetable stew. The latter was tiny and heavily spiced, yet it contained all those proteins and things. The former was pure carbohydrate – another large, hemispherical, plastic mass resembling ugali[6] in looks but failing to come up to par in taste.

The meal was the veritable dilemma. One couldn't eat what was nutritious and tasty but too hot, the curry-type food, without eating enormous quantities of this rather unpalatable, rubbery cassava. Furthermore this manioc, for the woman who cooked it, offered a second dilemma. Food gives one energy, yes; but one needed so much energy to pound and prepare this dish that one was unlikely to finish in credit. In the weeks to come, Baha grew to like it more, and in any case, for sixpence, he couldn't complain. His stomach did – the afternoon was punctuated by blow back noises. His evening meal, a plate of beans shared with schoolboys, didn't help. Fortunately, few heard him; the village band was performing. While one man banged out a basic rythm on sticks, a drummer and

60

a zylophonist supplied harmonies and tunes. It was a great noise and the musicians' agility was most impressive – the dextrous drummer drank beer synchronously. Meanwhile, the village menfolk danced joyfully; why, Baha knew not for there wasn't a woman to be seen.

Really, though, there was very little wild life seen around these parts. He saw one creature of note, an insect, and it was a beauty. Its abdomen was in coloured bands, bright enough to compete with Carnaby Street, while its transparent wings had the delicacy of Victorian lace. Apart from one stationary cameleon and many multi-coloured lizards which spent the entire day doing press-ups with their bright blue heads, the only other signs of game were a traditional animal trap, in which Baha received instruction, and the bush meat on sale in the dukahs[4]. And antelope is a dark, red, tasty meat; rather nice; but while one might relish in the stomach on such food, one cannot help a tear come to the eye on the beauty of wild life thus destroyed.

On the human side, life was also less wild; in South West Cameroun, where the bush had often been cleared for plantations of rubber or banana, they spoke English. For Baha, who had spoken only French or Swahili in December and January, this was great news. Soon he entered the Cameroun Highlands. Here, in the south and at low altitudes, the contours were covered in forest, and these steep foothills, through which many a crystal-clear brook babbled, offered some splendid views. Occasionally, he passed by a small coffee plot which sheltered under the trees. The plants were in bloom and the strong aroma from the white flowers was . . . . ah . . . . as advertised.

Everyday, Baha liked to chat with the local people but only if they also wanted to. The best way to know this was to wait for them to start. Some were very inquisitive, many were just friendly. Kids of course would look at anything unusual and shout a comment or two. Often they cried 'mzungu'[10] or the local equivalent. This, Baha was not particularly fond of. (When he shouted back 'African', they were sometimes most surprised). Here, in the Cameroun, he didn't mind so much for it was distinctly musical. It came out as a sort of 'maasaaleeleeleeleelee', emphasis on the first syllable. When uttered by lots of young, happy, unbroken voices, it was rather pleasant.

In Nigeria, a lot of kids were to say something like 'higheepo'.

Baha at first thought that this meant 'hello', so he 'higheepoed' back at them. They must have thought him perhaps odd. Later, he learnt the proper meaning: white man. No longer did he reply. No longer did he like the word. Hypocrite.

Another problem he was currently suffering from was that of personal cleanliness. Thrice in the Cameroun he was offered a bath. On two of these occasions, he had wanted a george before washing. His attempts to hide first were regarded as a little insulting – he never did learn the French word for 'george' – though as long as he came back and cheerfully jumped starkers into the stream or pool, all was well. Sometimes, his host for the evening would jump in with him. At other times, they just watched. One such Baha admirer – or was he just curious – kept on talking about 'flogs'. What flogs? Flogs what? It worried the naked Baha considerably until he remembered the Bantu[16] characteristic of mixing the 'l's with the 'r's. Ah ... no 'plobrem', though the 'flogs' were not particularly nice bath-mates. He wondered what they thought about the 'colorraly'.

Chapter 5.

ON, IN NIGERIA.

In Nigeria, Baha met a real bath-time dilemma. He rode down the brand new road to Calabar. Until a few years ago, this area had been just fairly open bush of small trees. There were a few villages connected by an age old pattern of dusty red paths. Now this road was not going to upset their traditional way of life as easily as all that; and every so often, across the smooth tarmac, was a dusty red footpath. Elsewhere, it was lonely.

Luckily the road passed by an old village at a stage when he was feeling in need of a rest. He stopped to buy a paw-paw and, while munching same, was asked to spend the night. Soon he was being led further away from the road having accepted the additional invitation for a bath. The village, he now realised, was much bigger

than he had at first imagined. Presently they came to the 'wash-house'. It was a large open pool which the entire village seemed to be using - old mamas, young kids, girls, boys, mothers and babies, the lot. Most of them were wearing but one piece of cloth. The complete scene looked rather like the washing rooms at Twickenham after the first ever international, inter-sex, interalia rugby match; interesting. Normally, on such occasions, Baha's eyes would wander at some considerable speed until they alighted on some bird's broad, black, bountifully beautiful bosom. (Actually, let's be honest, he normally did not witness such ablutions.)

On this day, however, he noticed that many pairs of eyes were not wandering. They were firmly fixed on this 'ere white man as he gingerly prepared himself for the bath. The water was filthy so nudity was no problem as long as one was in it, that is sitting down.

On what? But that was a minor problem. Most of the men, if naked, would just use a widespread hand, but a bashful Baha decided to keep his nickers on. In he went, to the upstream section (men always bathed upstream though in this particular pool, the current was minimal), and this bath passed without further embarrassment to either side, mainly because these villagers were not hampered by odd European ideas of modesty. They were just interested to see how a mzungu[10] was built; again, hairy legs and a festering chest might make the female mind boggle, or something. It should be added that, while the African girl sometimes does not bother about a bare bosom, she is invariably extremely modest below the waist.

Originally, he had intended to bathe that wound on his leg which had long since gone septic. However, when he saw the colour of the water, he replaced the rather soiled bandage - one load of bugs would be enough.

The evening finished well. He was served with fish soup, foo-foo[15] and plain boiled yams. Foo-foo, though it sounds like a deodorant, is actually a food prepared from yams. First the women pound it with large wooden poles of dubious hygiene in a fashion not dissimilar to the way Kenyan ladies molest their maize. Then it is boiled before being served as another 'putty-type' mass. It is, however, much nicer and less rubbery than cassava. Later, he was lulled to sleep by an odd combination: from his left came the rythm of the drums, to the right was a transistor.

The Nigerians in this part were very friendly. The women, some of whom were extremely beautiful (even when not bathing) smiled or even laughed their hallos. All called him 'Sir' despite his protests. All said "Welcome" most meaningfully. It was a pleasent atmosphere, though later it changed slightly for the worse. He came through areas of denser bush separated by huge palm oil estates to a bustling Calabar. In southern Nigeria, the townsfolk were often too busy to be friendly. Here, while awaiting the ferry across a river, he decided to have a shave. A small hotel allowed him an open-air, first floor balcony where a sink was fitted. The shave was successful but the nearby vultures, sitting on a roof but ten feet (3m) away, were a bit off-putting. The death of a two days' growth should not really have attracted such attention.

The road to Lagos was quite busy. The countryside consisted of fairly dense bush, sometimes, especially near the great rivers, becoming thick forest, sometimes breaking into open plains, often changing into a cultivated plantation. The gently undulating lands offered few views. The hamatan[14] made these fewer but it also, by diffusing the rays of the sun, kept Baha tolerably cool. The road passed through many villages. In one, a chap with mask, spear and musical accompaniment from the drums, came charging towards him. He gave Baha a nasty turn but all was in jest. In another, two little kids were pink! This puzzled Baha somewhat so he interrupted his lunch of bush fruit (fruit grown in the bush and which has no commonly accepted European name; in similar fashion, there is bush meat from antelopes, porcupines, monkeys and others), and asked. Apparently, after washing, their naked bodies were rubbed with this natural soft stone which was meant to keep them cool - the pinkness was purely by the way. His last question, "Are you hot?" the fruit seller decided she would not answer.

This area west of Calabar had some odd characteristics. Roadside graves were given to old chiefs and other dignatories; often they were structures containing pictures or even sculptures of the deceased. In nearby areas of Cameroun, homes had placed graves between their front doors and the main, or rather only, road - graves with headstones which looked like miniature verticle cross sections of Notre-Dame. South Nigeria's churches were plentiful. Most were Christian but of most varied demominations: one such was verbose indeed - 'Of the Grand Order of the Cherubim and Seraphim'.

Road-side dukahs[4] were everywhere; all sorts of foodstuffs were available and Baha's food problems were at an end; his own. There were traditional garis and foo-foos[15] and much conventional bread. Fruit, especially the citrus ones, were also plentiful, while plantains cooked in palm oil were superb. Fairly frequently, one would see a little dukah[4] selling palm wine - at three new and inflated pence; top wine, made from the taller palms, was a shade more expensive and effective.

In one 'bar', where he had actually stopped for food but had been mistaken, he was most warmly welcomed except, that is, by one man. All chatted in English freely but the exception spoke only in Ibo*. Baha countered by conversing with the others in English but, whenever this individual spoke, he replied in Swahili. Neither, of course, understood a word of what the other was saying. Eventually a compromise was reached. Baha didn't know Ibo but, because he was where he was, he should have done, if only for the sake of good manners. In turn, the Ibo did not know Baha's African language of Swahili. The compromise was a British one, and, despite that, successful; they decided to speak in English. They drank.

In fact, everything in this part of Nigeria was roadside. Beyond the roads and villages were many areas of bush, dense and virgin. (Ah, how often can these adjectives go together?) On the roads, many cyclists would come up from behind Baha and just stick on his tail. This, the knowledge that one was being followed, he found rather infuriating. There were exceptions; one was a gorgeous bird. On this occasion, Baha started the chatting, but she was more than just a pretty face. Her powerful legs soon had him panting - for both reasons - both legs? She won ..... hands down ..... of course. The second exception Baha saw was, for him, a most unusual sight - a mzungu[10] on a bicycle. The surprise was mutual. He was a Mexican. Also in Africa on bicycles were, according to various vague reports, a German, a Frenchman and a Japanese. It was nice to know one such idiot was British.

These days, Baha slept either in the country or in urban police stations. This was the first time since leaving Kenya that he felt confident enough to ask if he could camp in police grounds. Elsewhere, in Zaire for instance, such action might have led to

---

* One of the tribes, and therefore languages, of Nigeria.

endless questions, possible bribery, anything but security. In Nigeria, only assistance was received, though to be woken up at 3 o'clock in the morning to exchange addresses could have been interpreted as an alien gesture.

Invariably his bed was hard; either the earth under his tent or a concrete floor. In one of the police stations, in Benin City, there was no loo. He woke up in the morning desperate for the same. A rapid search was in vain. In a state of panic, he found two and a half bushes which could, he thought, just about provide adequate cover. He jumped in only to see, as his shorts descended, one of those vast, dual-tone spiders again. He dived out. A local saved the day. Indeed, though not just for this reason, most Nigerians he met were very warm hearted and several were amusing. One such differentiated between Americans and Britons.

"Yanks," she said, "tell you what they think you ought to know, while Brits say what they think you want to know."

She, like many other women, wore most fantastic headdresses. They wrapped one piece of cloth around their heads and, by subtle twists and turns, made it one or even two feet (60 cms) high. The men too were sometimes quite smart, wearing over western clothes traditional and colourful full-length gowns with contrasting 'night-cap' caps.

Often, cycling became a bit boring as when a road went straight through miles and miles of endless bush. Sometimes, especially on the new road out of Benin City, he was by himself with only his legs at work. His mind became dull. People, in villages and towns, invariably provided a bit of life. A few signboards perhaps were adequate. One showed the way to a 'Ministry of Welfare and Enlightenment'. Another warned that 'Anyone exceeding 5 m.p.h. will be dealt with militarily'.

Lagos itself was very colourful. People from all parts of Nigeria were there - the gowns and dresses were much more varied. It was busy. Everyone left the wide open spaces of Africa, it seemed, to come and get squashed on an island. Dukahs[4] were everywhere, their goods falling out into the streets. Cars too were numerous; most of them were stopped and hooting at the bloke in front who was in a similar condition. The noise was horrific. The heat was oppressive. Despite this, many people, Britons as well as Africans, were going to work in three piece suits or even pin-stripes. On the tortuous way in, they sweated and swore only to find in the office that the air-conditioning had broken down. Throughout the day it was the same, as many an excutive crawled nowhere by chauffeur-driven car. Meanwhile, in the markets, life on a much more musical note went on. And the open sewers continued to stink. Though the slums were cramped and dirty, the people who lived in and came out of them were remarkably clean and prettily dressed.

The same could not be said for Baha who arrived after many days without a bath or a change of shirt. He went to the office of a friend of his brother's but alas, the friend was up-country. The office was empty, save for an askari[13]. Baha was stuck. It was Friday afternoon and he only had ten shillings left, (his financial calculations in Nairobi had been somewhat optimistic). He therefore rang one of the other office workers from a list the askari[13] had, and asked if he could pitch his tent in their garden. He was invited to come round. On arrival he parked the bike and, tired and filthy, knocked on the door. It was opened by a superb leggy blonde.

"   ," said Baha. He was speechless. She too was rather taken aback but for different reasons. After some seconds of silence, he admiring, she glowering, she said,

"Er ..... would you like a shower?" Nine days later, after much kindness, many proteins, some visas and a few spare parts, he was ready to go again.

In one spare moment, on reaching a peak of naive enthusiasm, he decided to go along to the British High Commission to lodge a complaint against the Portugese government who had, in effect, stolen that canoe. The sum involved, £20, was not large when compared with most international figures but, Baha thought, principles were at stake; not only the one of Britannia's sinusoidal rule, but also that of theft. He was shown into an office. Opposite him sat a little fellow (about one inch taller than Baha) who, having heard the story, told him he was lucky to be alive. Baha, not having ascended all those stairs for just this piece of information, pressed the point. The fellow considered Baha an idiot, and that his problem was best left alone. He started to tell Baha of his own problems (which, in the confines of his air-conditioned office, did not seem unbearable), and also of the legal inadequacies of the case, especially as governments weren't really interested in principles, certainly not £20 ones, and nor was he. He would, however, forward the complaint to London. This, apparently, would cost about £25. Why, the uncivil Baha could not work out. Remaining as unsubtle as a pregnant elephant, he persisted:

"May I have a copy of the letter?"

"No."

Dejectedly he left, forcing his way out through airmailed newspapers and cocktail party invitations.

∞∞∞

"Why not remove your front mudguard?" his Lagos host asked. "It would make the bike lighter."

"That would be getting rather professional," Baha thought, "and if one gets too professional or fanatical about something, one tends to forget to enjoy it."

He cycled north, leaving just one thought for Lagos. Why not, one day, silence all horns, bells and other noisy devices which are carried by anything on wheels, and give one each to every pedestrian?

The road to Kano started in dense bush sometimes cleared for a little village and a dukah[4] or two. These would be selling citrus fruits. A meal of six grapefruit was pleasant, unlike the disturbances caused by chaps beating the life out of some bush fibres which as a result were reborn as sponges and backscrapers. The first breakfast on this leg was actually supplemented by a tin of beans; the local chief had heard of Baha's presence and was using this to serve as an introduction. This was only affected after a servant had approached, punctuating his gentle walk with many a bow from the waist and other salaams. Baha was indeed received royally. He was an interesting man who had spent some years in Britain and had liked the 'comfortable life'. His attempts at perpetuating a modified and tropical version of this appeared to be pretty successful.

Ibadan was a large city surrounded by small one-storey, shack-type houses and these stretched for miles in all directions. In between them, narrow roads and open sewers forced their way through while dukahs[4], spilling their goods everywhere, rendered the former almost useless for four-wheeled traffic; the latter also got blocked. The goods on sale were many; in medical stalls, one could get anything from aspirins to monkeys' skulls. According to the surgeon who removed a jigger* from Baha's foot, western and

---

* A small insect which penetrates the skin, lays eggs, and thus causes infection.

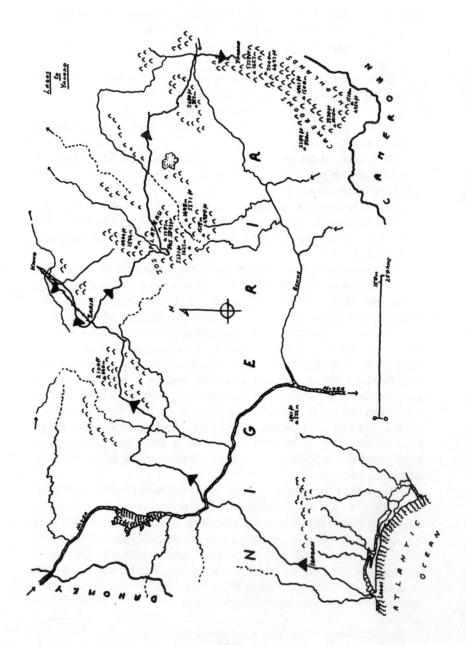

traditional medecines were, in their own way, equally effective. (Of course, monkey skulls were, as they say, not to be taken orally. Their use was similar, in a fashion, to that of flowers in a western hospital. During one of those idle moments in Kenya, Baha had tried some witch doctor's medecine made from the bark of a tree. The taste had born a very strong resemblance to those modern 'get-well-while-you-are-not-looking' cure-alls. And the resemblance had gone further: nothing had resulted from it.)

Gradually, life changed. The bush got less and less dense and, north of Ibadan, he started to see over long, flat distances again. The thinning vegetation shrank unto the horizon. He was now in the savannah; ah ..... that word with which in school, without ever knowing its meaning, he had lost and gained so many marks. It was a shade hot and there was little comfort in a gusty cooling breeze which was, as ever, a headwind. Occasional little 'bus shelter'-type, one-sided huts were in the fields to provide farmhands with a little peace from this hamatan[14], but Baha had no such solace.

North of the Niger he found many, more traditional villages. The pace of life was much slower, the people friendlier, the area more historical and the influences more Moslem. In the south, where Christianity and materialism were the rival gods (sometimes, as ever, both were accepted), many traditions have faded behind clouds of exhaust fumes. In the north, Islam was still strong and though this brought disadvantages economically and educationally, the old-fashioned way of life had much to be said for it. Little boys were often sitting by the side of the road, copying out extracts from the Arabic Qu'rān onto small tablets. The men ministered in the villages where the homes were of mud and, further north, straw. The women were at work and very much out of sight.

These villages were self-enclosed units, the walls of the huts often being linked to form a complete outer perimeter. Inside, each family had its own little area for its own belongings, one of the most important of which was the granary. In this part of the land, these were hemispherical (or hemi-egg shaped) mud nini[11] standing on dumpy little legs. From a distance, they resembeled magnified goats' udders; the goats, unabashed, slept in the compound by night, while by day they wandered among the fields. Such wandering for food was a full time job in these dry scrub lands, especially as the fields of groundnuts and maize had been fenced off.

It was here that Baha first experienced major language problems. When stopping for the night, he sometimes found a village in which no-one knew English, not even young boys (schoolboys would have been a misnoma). The only word of Hausa* he knew was Hausa; they knew but three words of English: 'me no (not know) English' - a confusing language.

Greetings could also be ambiguous. Often, men and women would bow or curtsey to each other. The one would ask many questions while the other would respond to each by the word 'marallah' (or something like that). Then the process would be reversed. In Britain, if we bother to greet each other, we do it pretty quickly with a 'how are you' to which, before reciprocating, we often fail to reply. In Nigeria - indeed many Africans took this human side of life very seriously - the greeting consisted in not only asking news of one's health, but also that of one's wife, job, kids, grandmother and Tom Cobbly. Each one was a seperate question. Each required its own answer. If all was well, the other, in a five minute conversation, would sound a bit like a railway engine working to rule: "marallah ..... marallah ..... marallah ...." Now obviously they could not greet the ignorant Baha this way. Instead, much to his initial alarm, they shook a clenched fist. By the look of it, a quick punch-up in the name of black power was imminent; but by the look of the eyes, all was well.

Despite these unforseen language problems, Baha, after making zzzzzzz noises and the like, was invariably allowed to spend the night. All he needed was a piece of earth for it was too hot to sleep inside the tent. Often he received more: a bucket perhaps to bath in. It was filled with water and then placed in the bucket room, a small circular wicker work construction about four feet (1.2m) high. It was rather nice to have one's bath while watching all the world, which couldn't watch all of you, go by. A wooden bed and even food might also be offered. One family was particularly generous; they even gave him one of those world-shrinking, soft drinks. He felt obliged to offer payment to his hosts who were far from well off. But this was refused. Muslims are known for their care of travellers. Their faith was indeed practiced.

---

* There were many Hausa tribes (and therefore dialects) as well as other peoples in North Nigeria. However, as a step towards national unity, one form of Hausa was becoming the official 'language of the north'.

Between Zaria and Kano, acres and acres of land were under guinea-corn though, at this time of year, the large furrows looked empty and barren while the rains were patiently awaited. Agriculture, nevertheless, was quite highly developed and this, surely, is one of the first signs of organised society. Elsewhere, some attempts at afforestation were taking place while the other side of the coin revealed efforts at clearing the land by fire. A few said this was to prepare the land for yams, some said it helped to kill snakes, and others to prevent fires! Sometimes these fires failed in their very purpose - by the roadside, Baha saw just one example of this: one charred skeleton of a telegraph pole which had been caught in the heat of the moment. In the forests, because of the dryness, the trees were far from dense, but this allowed the nomadic herdsmen to move their cattle easily in their perpetual search for water. Many of the rivers, for most months of the year, are just dry beds containing a small trickle of much used water. These, along with some isolated rocky outcrops, gave the scenery near Zaria more variety. Meanwhile, the heat was constant, the overhead sun overpowering.

One further food change on this northerly road was caused by the absence of the palm tree. His last glass of its wine was taken just north of Ibadan where he was shown the talking drum - it consists of two animal skins held by strings the tensions of which can be varied by squeezing with the left arm in the same way that a Scot torments his bagpipe. Meanwhile, the right hand wields a stick and beats. It is very musical and, in the old days, did indeed 'talk' messages. Further south, Baha had seen gourds used musically; some were adorned with beads and shaken, others were beaten and blown into.

While sipping this last glass of wine, he was told of an old tradition. A few people, after deeds especially noteworthy, acquired fame. As a mark of distinction, one front tooth was removed and this gap was, in time, regarded as a sign, not only of fame for the particular deed done, but of intelligence, wisdom and even beauty. Baha, who rather than risk a possible infection had had a front tooth removed in Nairobi (actually financial considerations had predominated), was now beginning to benefit from what the dentist's receptionist had regarded as anything but a sign of good looks. Just before Kano, on a particularly hot stretch, he stopped and sat under a wicker shade to have an orange or two. An old mama sharing the shade suddenly burst out laughing! Language problems hindered explanations but eventually he realised what it was - she had a missing front tooth as well but it was the first time she'd ever seen a mzungu[10] with such a defect/distinction.

Zaria and Kano are old cities with strong Arab characteristics, though with modern concrete structures appearing, influences of East Cheam are also seen. The older halves are full of character. They are walled, entry being made through one of a few broad and decorated gates. Inside are a conspicuous mosque, beautiful from without, rather empty within; an Emir's palace into which Baha was not allowed; and, in mud construction, a maze of houses, domed rooves, walls and alley-ways which meandered inexplicably everywhere. The walls rose periodically into little parapets. The doors often stood open; inside men rested or sat with a string of ninety nine beads which they used to recite the names of Allah, while boys learnt the Qu'rān. Little girls were often seen wearing lipstick on only the bottom lip. They and many boys had facial scars, while a few women were tattooed all over their chests and legs. Tribal traditions, even in the cities, were still strong. In Kano especially, one would see Hausas in their long, 'nightshirt' robes and their small, beautifully embroidered hats. These robes were not as colourful as those in the south, but the hats were definitely more so, especially those of the high officials, for in these silvers and golds were woven.

The Fulani, more often seen in the country with their cattle, wore large straw hats and carried swords like privates in a Chinese war-lord's army. The more northerly Taureq, famous for their horsemanship, wore large black turbans which left only their eyes to see and be seen. About their persons, they carried dirks, purses, 'sporans', all sorts of things. The spears they used to have were multi-purpose. With one end they killed; with the other, they rested the foot while riding or tilled the soil when not.

The city markets were fascinating. There, craftsmen made those little Hausa hats - definitely a man's job; others worked imported copper. On sale were hand carved gourds, earthenware pots, tablets of the Qu'rān, and many hand embroidered cotton garments. It was good to see, at the appointed hour, all trading cease while everybody, nearly, turned towards the East, knelt on the floor and prayed in loud monotones with lowered and humbled head. The ground, none too clean, was kissed. Soon, however, when the words of the prophet had been attended to, works unto profit continued. Non-Muslims, especially foreigners, sometimes complained when these followers of Islam suddenly stopped work to pray; lorries would halt, ferries would rest, machines would idle, the whole world would almost stop going round, though for little more than a few minutes. Meanwhile, in Portsmouth dockyard and elsewhere, work ceases twice a day while an ancient form of sun worship is performed with flags. (The British tourist guides only advertise Stonehenge.)

Here in Kano, as in so many Nigerian cities, the sewers were open. They all combined to form a pretty potent stream, the black 'waters' of which were poured onto the banks where tomatoes, carrots and other plants flourished. Out of the stench, as it were, came forth sweetness. Pure water, this far north, was scarce. Baha, still a hypocrite, swam in the mzungu[10] club swimming pool.

To cycle the odd hundred miles (160 kms) from Kano to Zaria, retracing his tyreprints, seemed rather masochistic. So he caught the train which should have arrived at the unfortunate hour of midnight. However, it was a late British train and it arrived at first light – perfect. Sleep for a time had been impossible while a blind man had been gently led from one end of the train to the other, singing at the top of his voice a' begging for alms. Every time the train stopped, kids, sometimes as if from nowhere, came to the windows selling food and water. One of the fruits resembled a raw tomato but only in looks. Its taste was very different and jolly good. Baha now understood why so many chaps in Kano had walked around with boxes of what had appeared to be completely raw tomatoes on their heads.

The road from Zaria was soon in the country, and all, well nearly all Nigerian roads were good ones. Here and there were vast open fields and small villages, the latter conspicuous because of the trees that surrounded them. The fields bore witness to the last harvest - sheaths of cereal stalks standing in cones some twelve feet (3.6 m) high. Occasionally, there were little highly cultivated areas fenced off from the goats while, if a stream was nearby, the lever and bucket system, as practiced in ancient Egypt and Kano's sewers, was used again for irrigation. Gradually, the road climbed up until it was on top of the Jos plateau. The vegetation, though intermittent, was getting stronger. The hills looked rugged, speckled as they were by formations of large, bare, rocky outcrops. Everything, especially this scenery, was more varied; for the first time in a week or two, he saw clouds - three little ones which failed miserably to hide that sun.

On his way out from Jos, he passed between two lines of hills, the silhouettes of which, by inscribing all known patterns, offered considerable beauty. The scene was a combination of greys and blacks, browns and yellows. Greens were few; dust was everywhere. Here, in a remote telecommunications tower watch post, he watched a fine sunset and spent the night. The next day, as happened quite often in various countries, a truck overtook only to then slow down and offer a lift. Baha usually refused these kind gestures. In this small pick-up however were two nuns. One, he thought, was possibly the matron from his old school in England, an establishedment which he had left some thirteen years previously. She was indeed. There followed an invitation to her mission and some highly medicinal orange juice. Delighted he was. For the time being, then, they parted.

Food by day was mainly biscuits and lumps of sugar cane plus one hot meal for, partially planned and partially by luck, he managed to pass through a large town roundabout lunchtime. It was usually rice. In the evening he was invariably in the country again; he sometimes ate yam flour and one of those small, 'blow-back', peppered dishes, and sometimes he ate not, for his stomach was complaining a little. Water was a problem. Many of the wells were running dry and the remaining contents were seldom pure. In one lonely homestead, he stopped and asked for a drink. There was a long delay. Eventually, a child climbed back up the hill with two pots. A cup full was duly given to Baha. He looked inside and there saw a brownish liquid. The 'see-through' test had failed. And it was foul! He failed to conceal his obvious dislike, his mouth grimmaced noticeably and the adam's apple rose in protest. He was then offered a second cup - ah ..... this one was definitely water, to see and to taste. The first cup, he now learnt, was one of millet water: water to which uncooked millet is simply added.

76

The road, leading as it did in a slightly southerly direction, showed gradual reductions in Moslem influence. The village huts, though still of mud, were of the more circular Bantu[16] type. In the bigger villages, schools were again seen, as were advertisements for various forms of booze. Old bottles full of a greyish liquid which Baha thought was possibly alcoholic were for sale. He only had one. In a more remote village, he looked in its small market for food. While passing behind some woman, he was almost physically stopped by the strong alcoholic smell emanating from large pots standing in front of her. This she noticed. Sign language for 'would you like a drink?' was readily understood. But was it strong? It had that 'I've-got-you-this-time' taste. He declined the second cup but accepted instead a smoke from an old man's pipe. That too was pretty potent.

In some markets, he was able to find little chai[5] dukahs[4] for almost the first time since leaving East Africa. Chai, to the British Baha, was almost essential. Here, spoons were not used; your tea was splashed ad nauseam from one cup to another, by which time most of the precious liquid was feeding the flies. As always, these were everywhere. From that point of view, one could indeed say that Africa was overpopulated. While these insects competed for your tea, kids jostled for your custom. Girls and boys carrying little plates of fruit, sweets or small buns hoped, pushed, even fought for orders; what a sad way for children to enter this competitive world.

Ahead, large hills jutted out of the otherwise straight horizon: promises of more varied and beautiful scenery. Since leaving the Jos plateau, he had travelled over flat or gently rolling plains. Some were farmed, more were virgin bush or denser forest whose trees, when compared to those nearer the coast, were small and rather dry looking. The rains were late.

Soon, some of the villagers were able to speak English again, but the cartographer's line between the Moslem north and the Christian south could only be dotted. In order to get to that mission, he had to branch off the main road. For the first time since Cameroun, he was on a long stretch of bad road. It was corrugated. It was sandy. And it, the other it, was hot. He was pushing once more. The tent poles were beginning to fall to bits, qualifying yet again for their adjective collapsible. Patience was fast disappearing. In one village where he stopped for water he obviously looked pretty tired. Water came; so did a pillow and a bed

77

mat. Back on the road, he hunted permanently for a bit that was smooth and hard enough for cycling. Otherwise he pushed. He was often on one side of the road or the other or indeed in the middle. Infrequent lorries and cars slithered about less and invariably stayed roughly in the middle, covering everything with sand in passing. One such did so twice. It was the police. It passed Baha, skidded to a halt, reversed somewhat sinusoidally in its own dust only to admonish Baha for cycling on the wrong side of the road!

"Yes Sir."

In yet more dust, it accelerated away. These conditions of heat, dust and no wind gave him his first experience of real thirst; it caused his bladder to ache and urine to be thick and deep yellow. To pee, which he had to do often though in tiny quantities, became itself painful. He was now in the northern part of the Cameroun Highlands. Amid rolling yam fields stood many little outcrops of dry and barren rock. In the distance, blue hills rose towards the sky. This area, until recently, was an almost forgotten part of Nigeria. Even now, some of the people were wearing just figleaves. At one point on the road, he passed many a chap armed with bows and arrows - they had formed a trap into which they had hoped animals would pass, not Baha.

The remoteness of these areas contrasted strongly with the ancient town of Maiduguri which laid to the north; from there, Nigerians, not then so called, had travelled across the Sahara to Cairo University at a time when no-one had heard of Oxbridge or the Ministry of Transport.

The mission stood next to a small village market where all sorts of herbs were on sale and where both men and women smoked pipes. He contemplated sampling yet another type of food (every time he saw something new and dead, he would have a go), but he changed his mind: it was soap. And what better day to arrive at an Irish mission than St. Patrick's day, unless, of course, one was thought to be, as Baha most certainly was, a British agent - a disturbing reflection on Britain's 'not-quite-so-glorious-as-in-the-text-books' history. Invariably, the former colonies tell a different, and truer, story. In the evening, Paddy was duly remembered though the liquid was one of those less traditional and more transparent beers.

The village was surrounded by yam fields, half of which remained fallow while the others were cultivated, and these

78

provided the main source of income. All the fields were ploughed by hand. So, when ploughing was due, much work had to be done. Each man's land was done in turn by everybody in the village, the work being speeded by the drummers. Meanwhile, that man's wife would brew up some beer (made from corn and stowed in large pots buried in the earth where it kept remarkably cool) and all would benefit after the day's labours. The next day would see another man's land ploughed, another wife's brew sampled.

'That,' thought Baha, 'is probably the best, certainly the most realistic form of socialism in the world. Private ownership is respected while all help all. Superb, as long as the missus can brew a decent drop of ale.'

In the mission, Baha witnessed for the first time a human birth. A fascinating and wonderful experience. It was good to know how one came to be. Previously, he had not realised how large a 7½ lb (3.4 kg) baby was. At his own birth, he had been over 12 lb (5.4 kg) - 'twas time for another letter to mum. The thing that struck him most was the bewilderment with which the child entered the world. His large round eyes immediately gazed in all directions - his mouth too tried to absorb some information - yet all this knowledge when it got to the brain meant so little for as yet he knew not how to think.

'Now when we get to heaven, we will still, according to most reports, have our capacities for thought with us. Though everything will be overpowering and infinitely strange, at least we will be able to think about it all.'

'Hallo Granny.'

Chapter 6.

MORE ON.

Staying at the mission was most enjoyable. His body was filled with vitamins, his mind relaxed by pleasant company and music. But he had to go. For fifty miles (80 km) or more, he was taken in the mission pick-up under strict orders of the good matron. Eventually, he was allowed to continue alone, and the worst of the sandy stuff was now behind him.

From the Cameroun border, which he reached after three days, there laid a distance of about a hundred miles (160 km) during which he would be penniless and centless, for only at Garoua would he be able to cash a cheque. In the meantime, he was on rough roads, without a pump, in a rather lonely part of the world. It was hillier country and any signs of life were only to be found in the valleys. All the views, however, were now much more expansive. The season of hamatan[14] was at an end. On the hills, rugged black rocks gave a forbidding look. There was little vegetation, the trees were without leaves. Down below, in the more fertile valleys, the villagers were collecting tall, dried grass to renew the roofs of their mud houses. The rains were expected shortly. What little agriculture there was thrived in small fields fenced off by cactus plants. In the villages, a few chaps were quietly spinning cotton. Outside one house, while he was going down a rather steep and tricky track, he was greeted by a local playing a three foot (90 cms) long wooden horn. His dance was gay, if not a little menacing.

He spent that night in a little village of about six huts; its income was mainly from selling firewood (not a good industry to have when on the fringe areas of drought, but what else?). He was offered a chicken. Fantastic. Having no way in which to repay, he tried, by sign language, to refuse. But when he saw that this would cause offence, he happily accepted. It was very fresh, and definitely free range - superb. And that food saved him from the pangs of hunger. It took all of the next day to reach Garoua, coming down a long broad valley through these dark, almost canyon-like hills. Many little streams, some dried at this time of year, wandered down to the main small river at the bottom. Over the centuries, each had worn away the hard rocky earth; though the geological causes were the same, each steep valley was impressively different.

Gradually, the sides became less steep, the hills lowered, and the plains started. Then, at Garoua, he was allowed, just, to stay at the local mission school. Still, at least he got shelter for the night and that really was all he needed; well nearly all. He asked for the loo, but obviously at the wrong moment.

"Où est loo?" he said, hoping for a 'loo est là'. But

"Ooh lala!" was all he received before the père went off in a huff. Perhaps his French was still far from perfect. In the church was a novel instrument - a zylophone with, under each bar, a resonating chamber or, to use the local word, a gourd. Tuning must have been a problem.

The next morning, having bought some money and eaten much, he headed south, bridging the Benue river for the third time. He was now armed with a new 'water-bottle'; proper ones had been available but expensive, so Baha had settled for an old car oil-bottle. He washed it, but obviously imperfectly as a sludge remained. In fact, it was not until Kinshasa that he managed to get it properly cleaned. For the coming weeks, its contents, water from dubious sources, tasted much, and not nicely. The Benue, because the rains had not yet come, was a small stream in a vast river bed, the emptiness of which waited patiently for the flood. Here, as at the other two crossings, women washed clothes, children splashed, and cows watered and were watered. One would suspect the presence of pollution perhaps, but, generally speaking, those hardy, downstream Nigerians had looked healthy enough. The sick, of course, a layman doesn't see, not only because hypochondria is rare. The peoples here were very similar to those neighbours, both ethnically and in their Islamic religion though, in the rural areas certainly, the Camerounians were poorer. In fact, Baha went through two villages without even noticing them. In a third, unmarked on his map, he spent a night. Again he had a bath in a bucket in a basket, and admired the passing maidens. A bamboo bed was prepared for him. There was of course no mattress, but twenty or so straw mats were a comfortable, itchy substitute.

The roads, for the most part, were now pretty good and getting better. In those bits not yet replaced by modern laterite surfacing, however, there were deep ruts hidden under a thick coating of fine, orange dust. Often, Baha was in it up to his knees. The road travelled across a large, gently undulating landmass. The vegetation was slowly getting thicker and the bush was now dense enough for animals. He was in game park country. He recalled to mind those Zairois hippos. Locals spoke of elephants and lions. In this park, the road, the only one going south, formed just the perimeter. There was no safer alternative. For two days his eyes were sharp, his ears silent, waiting ..... excitement, tension, pulse, fear .....

He saw a squirrel. And even that was on the wrong side of the road, out of the park.

Later on, however, he met some other wild creatures - tsetse flies. These usually stuck close to the trees but where the trees stuck close to the road, they stuck to Baha. He tried everything in his possession: mosquito sprays, trousers, anoraks; all were in vain. They bit. Bit by bit, bite after bite, Baha became perforated. He was delighted to come to a village, a clearing, and therefore freedom from these pests. He rested under a mango tree and ate its fruit. But for the mangoes being in season, he would have been in trouble - this was now his fourth consecutive meal of fresh, juicy mangoes only. 'Twas just as well his beard had been removed.

After a long push over some hills, a great circle of which contained the source of the Benue, and a night's sleep on top of them, he reached the big town of Ngaoundéré where he was able to stock up. As usual, the African restaurants sold the popular foods. Baha was most surprised to learn that Camerounians have taken a strong fancy to macaroni. Delicious. This town, like Garoua before it, had a very comfortable looking residential area for 'les blancs' (Europeans) while elsewhere there were rows of rectangular, Moslem-type mud houses. Even without those open sewers, these towns were much cleaner than their Nigerian counterparts. In their markets, colour was added from great lengths of cloth; many men wore full length shirts.

South of Ngaoundéré were rolling hills. The greenery was much thicker. The soil was red again, and the chickens were fatter. Bananas, cassava and sisal were growing. One was back in shamba[1] country. The homes were often of circular mud construction with very thick straw thatch giving the homes a 'trog'-like appearence. In the villages, especially the more Moslem ones, the homes were linked to the communal wall. Entrance was made through a large 'foyer' hut. This was taller than the others with a great 'hairier-than-thou' thatch. But it contained only two doors, one out to the street, one into the compound.

Occasionally there were stalls selling meat and fruit. In the former, killing and certainly chopping up were done on the spot. Dogs, crows and numerous flies competed for bits, though not much was thrown away. Kids often gave a helping hand. For them, there was nothing unusual in an eight year old boy carrying on top of his own head, a recently dead cow's severed skull, holding it, of course, by the horns. From behind, the great, blood-red cross section of the dripping neck persuaded Baha to stick to fruit. What nicer than a meal of avocados. In another village, he stopped for lunch. A sip of the beer was more than enough - ugh! He ate the only thing available, bread and meat, under the watchful eye of a large landlady who wore three rings, one in each ear and the third in her nose.

Later he saw a ring in a bull's nose; one obvious indication of a French type mzungu[10] farm. Europeans, having no lions except those concrete ones on public buildings, tend to regard the bull as a somewhat ferocious beast. In Africa, where alternatives are many, he is just treated like a cow – well, for most of the time. On the whole, however, the expatriate tended to stay in the towns working in offices and shops. In the latter, the 'madames' carefully supervised the cashiers' tills.

At Meiganga, he stayed at the mission and took a day of rest. After more macaroni, much rain - his first since Zaire - some washing and one puncture - his first for over one thousand miles (1600 km) - he treated himself to a tin of margarine to go with his bread. The result of such sudden luxury was diarrhoea ..... again. And this, on the corrugated roads which followed, was no joke. At least his bike and tent poles weren't falling to bits any more; thus his temper was definitely more controlled. And he was now en route for the Central African Republic's border. The greenery was continually getting taller and thicker. One or two villages lined the route; in these, the houses were just placed haphazardly. The Moslem influence was no more. Baha usually aimed to have his lunch in a village, primarily because insects therein would be fewer unless, of course, one was in a butcher's dukah[4]. To-day, however, his stomach was faster than his legs - while in a village, nature called him to the bush. He stopped in what looked like a pleasant spot, having first answered the call, to eat his mid-day meal. He sat down and started on the first mango, but the chosen seat was on top of a family of ants. He moved only to be plagued by flies, but there was no point in trying to out-manoeuvre these fellows. They were very annoying. He tried the old colonial technique of killing a few as an example to the others, but that didn't work either. He was distracted for a time by a fantastic noise from about a hundred yards behind him - some monkeys were having a fight, or a funny sort of game, in a nearby tree; but still there was the problem of how to eat a lunch without sharing it. He gave up.

He continued along a ridge which ran between two sweeping valleys. But clouds, cumulous and ominous, gathered. The day's rain storm caused him to stop a shade earlier than usual. He was offered a disused hut, the roof of which was of airtex and grass. The rain soon explained its emptiness. But one old boy offered him a bed in his own hut - a room full of large earthenware pots and carved calabashes which were used for water and butter respectively. The next day, after a good meal of macaroni which he rightly suspected would be his last for some time, he crossed the border. Here the roads were much emptier; probably just as well for there were three major puddles that were the only obstacles for miles. Baha dismounted and walked through the first, gained confidence; rode but slipped in the second, fell, lost some; rode and fell again, hard, in the third one. lost the remainder. The bike crashed to the ground. He gashed his thumb, jumped up and down in pain, and slipped yet again to finish up, or down, on his bum in another pool of mud.

The rest of the road was, in comparison, dry and solid. Along the verges, for some miles now, were many groups of large toadstools. They were about the size as those depicted for the use of leprachauns:

'Ah ha. Now there's another good excuse for an expedition. Perhaps that will help to reduce the number of thetis-writing undergraduates on Kenya's palmy and leggy beaches.'

The road to Bouar came to the edge of a line of hills. From these, the land fell away into a great plain of thick vegetation. In the distance were more hills. The view was breath-taking. It was impossible to absorb all the beauty in one fleeting glance. He stopped, sat by the roadside, ate some bananas and bread (a combination to which he had grown very partial), looked, admired and absorbed. He then desended into this thick woodland, the first real signs of the Zaire river basin again, and cycled for many an hour before rising onto the southern tip of those previously distant hills where the town of Bouar majestically sat. Another day had passed. Needless to say, the commissariat, whatever that was, sat in a commanding position overlooking not only the plains but the town as well. Here Baha had to go and wait for a small formality but, with those breath-taking, banana-consuming views, it was not an unpleasant one.

What were not so pleasant, however, were the townspeople who started calling 'touriste, touriste,' again.

"One doesn't mind the kids so much, for after all they have no toys. But it's a bit off when grown-ups start shouting these slogans as well. I mean chaps with tans on Westminster Bridge wouldn't like passing Brits to be shouting 'immigrant, immigrant'."

Baha thought of a few replies but, remembering the strong military presence in the country, decided to remain silent.

In comparison, as ever, the villagers were very friendly. It was superb at the end of the day to sit on a small 'deck-chair' (two intertwined planks of wood which 'collapsed' into a seat) and watch the sun set over green and distant hills. The red of the sun faded, only to be superseded by the glows of many little fires set against the silhouette of the huts before these in turn were enhanced by the brightness of the tropical moon. The villages sat in cleared bush; again the ground was dried mud. And yet again it appeared that most of the villages were clinging parasitically to the main road. Elsewhere was virgin bush.

Cassava and groundnuts were now the basic foodstuffs, while chickens and goats provided meat, but rarely eggs or milk, respectively or not. The cocks and hens had little huts on stilts built for them. In these they slept peacefully, protected from snakes and other beasts of the night. The goats tended to just stand in a bunch in the middle of the village, relying more on their numbers. By day, the animals wandered everywhere with their usual quantity of unnecessary noise. The cocks, of course, started their 'cock-a-doodle-ooh's' at about four o'clock and, regrettably, they didn't consider their day's work done by dawn. Many villagers accepted the din. Kids however, lacking patience and past-times, often hurled projectiles at the wretched beasts, stifling thereby many a 'doodle-ooh'.

In another village, he paused. Not far from the roadway were many people dancing in an endless circle while others stood beating the drums - drums which were highly decorated cylinders some three feet (90 cms) high. Some of those present, the more elderly and the kids, sat on the periphery entranced, like gazelle in the headlights, by the vibrating rythms. The dancers, on top of their dresses or trousers, were wearing little bundles of leaves - 'twas obviously a traditional occasion. One dancer waved to Baha urging him to join in. He hesitated. A passer-by explained that it was a funeral.

"But," said Baha thinking his leg was being pulled, "why are they all looking so happy?" Silly question.

Further on, he saw some really sad individuals. They approached and asked if he had heard that the French President* was dead. Initially he said no, latterly yes, but never at any time did he appreciably change his countenance. This puzzled them. Perhaps however, if thay had known that Baha was a Brit and an anti-common-marketeer, such apparent disinterest would not have shocked them. Even so, their attitude surprised him. He found it difficult to conceive Brits let alone Kenyans mourning a cold Harold or a dead Ted**.

On the Saturday, he hoped to find a mission. He stopped to eat a breakfast and ask a question but, as sometimes happened, they did all the questioning. 'Why not go by car?' was a fairly regular one. 'Why haven't you got a watch?' was another. In answer to the second, he pointed to the sun.

"Right," they said, "What is the time now?" So, here was the test. Baha flicked his hand up to the horizon, made an impressive little gesture or two, wondered what time zone he was in and replied, using his pigeon French,

"A quarter to eight." They immediately rushed to find a timepiece. To estimate the hour was clever but to estimate the quarter? One lonely chap with a watch was almost assaulted; sixteen minutes to eight. All, including Baha, were most impressed. In jest, he asked for payment. No more questions.

He duly found the mission and there, by the local well which was not too near the public footpath, he washed everything. It was again time for a complete change of clothes - all three of them. As he was only two days out of Bangui, he decided to forgo his day of rest and so, after church and a visit to the local water falls, he continued on what should have been, but was not, a better road.

* George Pompidou.
** Harold Wilson and Ted Heath, Britain's alternating premiers of early '74.

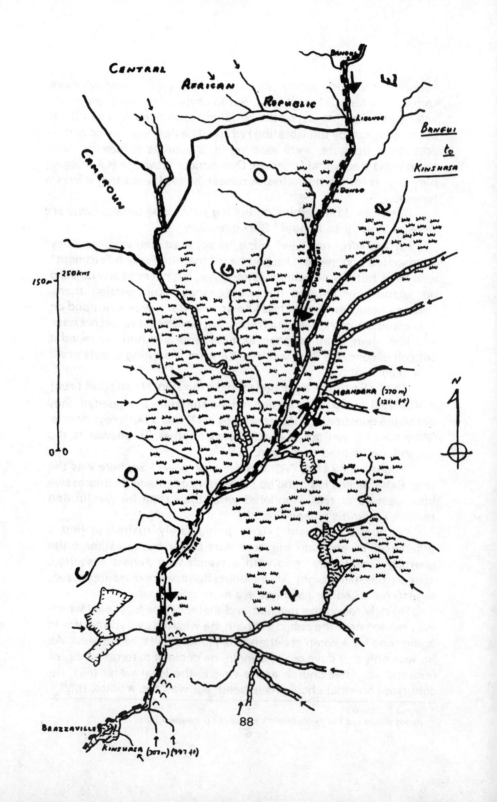

CENTRAL
AFRICAN
REPUBLIC
CAMEROUN

BANGUI

UBANGE

DONGO

BANGUI
to
KINSHASA

OUBANGUI

MBANDAKA (370 m)
(1214 ft)

CONGO

ZAIRE

BRAZZAVILLE

KINSHASA (307 m) (997 ft)

250kms
150m

0 0

N

Chapter 7.

SORRY MUMMY.

In southern Nigeria he had seen a few snakes, mainly dead and in the middle of the road. In the north, he had seen but two monkeys. Indeed, in the last couple of months, apart from birds, he had seen very little game.

Before reaching Bangui, he had decided he would travel from there by boat to Kinshasa. His legs needed a rest, and he needed the variety. He was a little surprised to discover, on arriving, that all boats were laid up and would remain so until the rains filled up the river to a sufficient level again.

This was a blow. He had, so he calculated, four alternatives. He could go by road; this was quickly dismissed because it would take him back towards Kisangani which he had no wish to revisit, and because he now knew what Zairois roads could do to bicycles. Secondly, he could wait for the rains but, at an estimated two months, this idea was also quickly discarded. The third alternative was panic; this he knew he could do to the very letter, including the first. Lastly, he could buy a canoe.

Now he had received a letter from his Mum after the Cabinda affair which gave pretty clear instructions as to what not to do: buy canoes and visit game parks. In this case however, he felt he would be forgiven partially because he would otherwise be stuck and partially because he was strictly river bound. There were no Atlantic rollers to conted with; the current was in one definite direction only; navigation was, in theory, no problem; and, as the saying goes, it would be all right in the end. In any case, he could rejoin the road at Libenge if something went drastically wrong.

So, after a night on the sands with some chaps who were travelling across Africa in the back of a lorry, he went to buy a dug-out canoe. He thought his powers of bargaining were much improved when he finished in possession of one for only £8. A small shauri[7] over paddles followed. In the light of his previous experience, he bought two and lashed the handles together. Then, having stocked up with fruit (his earlier attempts at stocking up had failed completely - a double meal of rice and fish had ended in

89

vomit) and loaded his bicycle, he pointed the bows downstream and set off, hoping his as yet unscheduled grandchildren would all, in time, be suitably impressed. It was about 3 o'clock.

He soon realised that he had 'been done'. The damned thing was built in the shape of an elongated 'S'. As soon as it started to turn, one way or the other, it was nigh on impossible to correct it. Either he had to stop everything, repoint and start again, or he had to let it do a complete revolution. He stopped for a cargo shift in which he hoped his torso would act like a sort of mizzen, but it didn't help very much. Still, he was going downstream, albeit rather slowly, and that was the right direction. To go back was not only against his principles but, because of this useless propulsion system, impossible. Never was a dug-out more so.

During the previous evening on the sands, many subjects had been discussed. Apparently, on their travels, this lorry load had come across some old ammunition stores only partially hidden in the Zairois jungle - an aftermath of the civil war.

Bangui was still in sight, just. Suddenly, from somewhere ahead, there was a mighty roar. Baha turned and saw, but thirty yards ahead, a dark domed something with two horns submerge.

'A mine!' he thought, recalling the previous evening's conversation. But he was puzzled; he knew mines could bob up to the surface but they didn't normally bob down again.

Suddenly once more, there it was a second time. It broke surface and roared. The horns wagged! Horns wagged? Mine roared? Ah! 'Twas alive. It was a hippo, and an aggravated one. Obviously, man was not wanted. Its home was being threatened. (Up hippopotamus lib.) It dived again, presumably in preparation for an attack. Baha panicked; he stopped, back-paddled furiously, rammed himself aground and jumped onto dry land!

A lonely fisherman, appearing from nowhere, comforted him and explained - how Baha can't remember because he knew not French nor Swahili - that hippos don't like being disturbed but that if one stuck close to the bank, one would be OK. He also added that there weren't any more downstream. Slowly, his heart thumping a little less severely against his ribs, he built up sufficient courage to re-enter the piroque[17] and set paddle once more. Although he frequently looked over his shoulder, he didn't see the beast again; a beast which, afterall, was probably only a mother fighting to protect its baby, all umpteen hundredweight of it.

He paddled on, passing between a few buoys where the river narrowed and the stream showed itself to be quite strong. Slowly, Bangui passed from view. He paused for a mango or two, and gently drifted downstream. He felt happier. Just before sunset, the wind blew up rather strongly from ahead so much so that any drifting done was backwards. He parked on a sandbank, leant back on his rucksack and slept awhile. He was now, officially as noted in his passport, in Zaire. The river Oubangui acts as the border between Zaire and, firstly the Central African Republic, later Congo Brazzaville. So whenever Baha stopped, he aimed for the left bank. The other problem was the old one of his Zairois visa being valid for only a month. It's a big country and a canoe is a rather slow mode of transport. He resolved to continue his journey by moonlight.

Sure enough, at about midnight, the half moon came up. When all was tolerably bright, he set off. The wind had died; it was flat calm. He paddled or just drifted. At one stage, after a quiet doze of unknown duration, he woke with a bang - he had drifted into a sand bank, the vertical walls of which led to Baha's imagination achieving immediate increased productivity before he had regained full consciousness. The river was now much broader, the current weaker and sand banks were everywhere. His journey was often brought to a temporary halt. Thus, despite it being all downhill, he still had to do some pushing; the canoe was heavy indeed; paddling the piroque[17] was often punctuated by paddling of the Brighton fashion.

On his travels, Baha usually woke at first light. This morning, however, he was awake for the complete dawn; its chorus, there in the middle of the jungle, was really quite something - an amazing cacophony. Among the many living noises, he could discern frogs and geese, he could see hovering kingfishers and those hornbills (he thinks they were hornbills) which, despite centuries of evolution, still couldn't fly properly. On the downhill straight they gathered speed, then, folding their wings, they assumed a streamlined posture and pointed themselves skywards in order to gain height. They quickly slowed down. The wings were spread to prevent gravity taking charge but they'd already stopped. They started downhill once more. They had much cause to shreik.

With the first light of day, he saw other canoeists. All, at this hour, for some unknown reason, were female. By the look on their faces, Baha was a rare sight. Ah, 'twas good to be well off the tourist drag again. Later, men were also 'at river'. Some fished, by net or harpoon; some, with wife and kids, travelled with firewood or fish to market, a journey of perhaps three days.

This canoeing, even with the double paddle, was hard work. The sun, vertically overhead, was merciless and, out in midstream, there was of course no shade. Nor was there a cooling breeze;

indeed, there wasn't an isobar for miles. He rested often, leaning back on his rucksack and reading a book. At least water was no problem, though for the first time, having carried them for a few thousand miles, he decided to use his sterilizers - the water type. Afterall, lots of chaps and animals did lots of describable things in these rivers. A pee from a hippopotamus, in this the dry season, constituted a fairly high level of natural pollution.

He stopped in a village to buy a complete bunch or branch of bananas - yet again, his dietry choice was a little limited. He also received some reports of more hippos and even crocodiles. To Baha's anxious questions which quickly followed, some replied 'oui', others 'non'. He gave up, and resumed paddling until the sun plopped into the trees whereupon he found another suitable, left-handed sandbank. When the moon rose, he set off for his second moonlight cruise - the bike was poor company. Now in coming to the left hand side of the river, he had obviously moved out of the main stream. It took quite a lot of pushing and shoving before he could get going in the deeper water again. By the time he was drifting nicely, a great cloud was approaching from the East, intent on cutting off the moonlight. It succeeded. But Baha continued - in this the twentieth century one couldn't allow a mere power-cut to disrupt life. Soon, however, he realised that this cloud was not only bringing darkness. There was a mighty roar which reached for a crescendo as the tropical rainstorm approached. A wall of water came out from over the forest. Whoosh! It bucketted down. Luckily he saw a couple of lights ahead on yet another sandbank. He paddled fast. He was soaked. The piroque[17] was filling up fast though with his baler/shaving bowl/drinking cup, there was little actual danger of sinking. However, he was very wet and cold. He beached the canoe alongside some others, and then ran towards these little lonely lights. Each was in one of two small huts made of straw and leaves on a light frame of sticks. He stuck his head in at one of the open ends and asked for shelter. It was barely seven feet by five on the ground, and just four feet high (2.1 x 1.5 x 1.2m). On one side were six fishermen, on the other a family. It must have been about half past two in the morning.

"Entrez," they said. What was one among so many? He climbed in, as instructed, on the side of the six. While disturbing everybody, he noticed the family was a man and his wife with a child kept warm inbetween them. Presumably it didn't always receive such a comfortable position, nor, for that matter, did the six fishermen! There, in this little hut, with the wind constantly blowing through, he spent the rest of the night, shivering a lot but sleeping not.

By morning, the rain had reduced to a drizzle. Positively the least he could do, after such hospitality, was to give everyone what they obviously wanted - a malaria pill. He set off again, rejoining the main stream, leaning on a very wet rucksack. He decided that he had had enough of this night sailing. On this day, it was now damp and delightfully cool. Occasionally company encouraged him to increase speed a little; the locals were definitely much faster. And the rain discouraged reading. Some of these riverfolk were, considering their circumstances, quite sophisticated. Or was it perhaps that Baha's French was not? Often, their first question was,

"Vous êtes Anglais? (Are you English?)"

He was gradually working out the navigational system used in the river. The buoys he could understand, but these were few. The other marks were white arrows or lines nailed to trees on the river banks. Their meaning, once deciphered (it took a day or two) was tolerably straightforward. Towards this evening time, however, he became confused again. It had just stopped raining and visibility had cleared a little. There were buoys, beacons and arrows everywhere and, in the middle of them all, one tug which was completely high and dry on the rocks. Everything was suddenly there; he realised what was happening. He was entering some rapids, and it was too late to turn round. The main stream twisted to the left and right. Then, just ahead of him, bubbling menacingly between silent black rocks, was the main rough bit, about fifty yards long. The stream, less than ten yards wide, was fast. It was noticeably downhill. The waters were choppy, and those waves were definitely higher than Baha's undulating gunwhale.

'Still, if we're quick enough .....' He barged through, paddling furiously to keep her straight and fast, and happily he came out, wetter, but the right way up and on top. All rather exciting - afterwards.

And with that, the rain returned and night came. He stopped in a small river settlement where he was given a nightwatchman's open bamboo shelter for the night. For this he was grateful, 'cos the rain grew harder, the ground softer. When he awoke, he noticed a man looking at him. Er ..... it was a rather damp looking nightwatchman. Baha offered him a banana - a small price for peace.

In the evening after a further day's paddle, he camped on yet another sandbank, this time opposite Libenge. His neighbours sold him a grilled fish which, except for the eyes, was rather good. But those eyes were like solid marbles which played cheekily amonst Baha's missing teeth. In the morning, he paddled over to the town side in order to buy food. By the banks, mothers washed and children played; by beating their palms on the flat surface of the water, they produced a most credible rythm, until other drummers upturned them.

In the market, he spied another large bunch of bananas. His mind did a quick calculation before he offered the old mama who sat behind them so many nini[11] for the complete bunch. She, seventy if a day, moved like the proverbial flash of greased lightning. Before he knew what had happened, the money was out of his hand and the bananas were in. 'Done!' She, as joyful as the spring(that untropical phenomenum) and almost as sprightly, danced away. He

94

did his sums again. She had made a good eighty percent extra profit.

It was here that Baha was told, over a glass of palm wine, that boats were running from Dongo, a further sixty miles (96 km) downstream. So he decided to continue paddling down to there, but certainly no further. Thoughts of paddling all the way to the river Zaire were no longer entertained. Thinking Easter, April 14th, could be celebrated in the next town, and hoping it would be more enjoyable than his abortive Christmas, he lost little time and set off, though owing to the island some ten miles (16 km) long opposite Libenge, he was once more out of the main stream, and drifting speed was reduced.

Progress was slow. Fellow canoeists, on overtaking, chatted happily. An old man offered him a complete bucket of cockles - one was enough. Another guided him safely round some hippo pools. They only saw the animal tracks - large troughs in the sands where stomachs had ploughed through on their way to a night of grass. With him, Baha conversed at some length; both were equally surprised to hear the other had been deep in Nigeria. Communications with another traveller consisted of only a wave - he was definitely one of the original fishermen wearing but one simple piece of cloth which passed under his crutch before being tied at either end to a string waistband. What one would call an i-front, no doubt, or an i-back.

By evening time, he had rejoined the main stream. He camped opposite a small fishing village - a line of thickly thatched, large, rectangular huts separated by bananas and palms, all dwarfed by the surrounding jungle. From the top of a bank some twenty feet (6m) high, they looked out over the river, sometimes a mile or so wide. Below there were many a piroque[17] for fishing. Some of these villages were really quite sophisticated relying not only on fish but also on palm oil, cassava, coffee, maize, bananas, guavas and mangoes.

The sun descended, and he nipped round a corner for a george. It was solid! Wow! For the last few months, he had had general stomach troubles if not complete diarrhoea. It had started in Cameroun in early February when he had eaten too much African food, in particular those 'blow-back' soups; it had continued in Lagos with the change to much superbly rich European food, principally because he had been unable to say no; and it had lasted to Bangui because of the suspect waters he had drunk. Now at last, at long last, his guts seemed to be working properly again. What more could a man ask for as an Easter present.

Actually diarrhoea, from the point of view of stores, was not a good ailment. He carried a few medecines for same, but loo paper had long since been classified as an unnecessary luxury. One of his other store problems, however, concerned reading material. Books were essential. Before leaving Nigeria, he had had to stock up with sufficient English books to get him to Zambia. A compromise solution to these two stores problems was perhaps inevitable. Any book he considered useless, physically and/or literally, he would use at and unto the end, twice, as it were. One such book, by one of those particularly verbose American authors, solved his reading problem from Bangui to Mbandaka, and his rear end problem from Bangui to the very end - Nairobi. It was his bog book; a happy ending.

At one particular stage, when his diarrhoea had been very bad, he had had to struggle to keep his reading ahead.

Easter itself, like Christmas, was no day of celebration. On his way downstream, he nodded off to sleep and was carried by a back eddy into a lonely part of the river - thus, more pushing was required. He arrived at a town at about mid-day, late. He parked his canoe on an enormous sandbank and started walking, barefoot, to the town. It was hot. The sands were like one enormous hot-plate. Soon, he couldn't walk because of the heat on the soles of his feet. He had to stand, half naked, on his shorts until his feet were cool enough to attempt another ten paces. He nearly spent the entire afternoon marooned on the sands. He eventually got to the end of the sandbank, only to discover it was an island. Thus he had to walk all the way back again and paddle right round it before he was able to step ashore - with his shoes on. He got to know this sandy bit of Africa quite well; he passed a few fishermen who, using just a long string to which were tied occasional shells and some bits of grass, were catching many little tiddlers in the warm, shallow pools of this sand island.

He strolled into town. The church was shut. There was no evening service. The market was closed. One shop sold him a tiny tin of tomato juice for a shilling. No eggs. Happy Easter. He walked back.

Actually, he rode back on a local cyclist's luggage rack.

Hanging on, on these rough roads while the rider was swerving to avoid ruts, stones, pedestrians and policemen, was difficult. At this end of a bike, Baha was definitely a beginner.

He set paddle. It was raining lightly. A few miles further on, he decided to pitch tent. The sun was now desending through the clouds. Rigging the tent with this wind blowing was difficult. Orange hues were fanning upwards from the west. The damned sand was useless for tent pegs. The clouds to the east were littered with reds and golds. The tent collapsed. The last lights of the sun danced their final waltz in the upper branches of the trees. Blast! Beautiful. Idiot! Peace.

He did eventually, with some help, get it up. It was a gorgeous night. He slept outside.

Bank Holiday Monday was again hot. Earlier, whilst on the road to Bangui, he had lost a hat for the third time. Because of their short duration, his latest was just a cheap scarf, but in this heat it was not enough. While the scarf covered his head, two handherchiefs were tied over his peeling nose, and his anorak protected his legs. Paddling and reading were thus still possible.

He spent just one more night on the sands, again in the company of fishermen; they gave him two fish. In the darkness, he didn't realise, until he started on the bigger second one, that they weren't fillets. By this time, he had eaten fish, flesh, fins, heads and tails as well as a few bones. He also ate three of the four 'marbled' eyes. And thus, with only one further small obstacle to be circumnavigated, an unidentified hippo whose back was above surface in the middle of a narrow buoyed channel, he reached Dongo. In the small port warehouse was the 'chef du collectivité'*, who gave him a beer.

In the market were lots of mangoes and much cassava, precooked and wrapped in leaves to make sausage type nini[11] anything up to three feet (90 cms) long. One could carry them slung over the shoulder; when hungry, one just untied the end and bit off a mouthful. And for two days, while waiting for the official boat, he lived on this and more dried fish. This ready-to-serve, wrapped cassava quickly differed from its fresh rubbery form. It dried, and became greyer, more solid and, surprisingly, yet more unsatisfying. One could eat vast quantities of this more eatable and less edible mass without noticeably getting full.

* A twentieth century village headman.

One sight amused him rather. Early one morning, some piroques[17] were being slowly paddled upstream by a team of three women, standing in evenly spaced positions along the canoe's length. These females, definitely up to Oxbridge weight standards, were buxom. They were wearing three piece dresses consisting of a wrap-around skirt, a short blouse and, on top of the former, a grass skirt! They formed a fair sight as, leaning down from the hips to plunge the blade in for yet another stroke, large pot bellies fell out from under the blouses, only to be heaved back into position on the vertical stroke. What a team! In .... out .... Or perhaps, out .... in .... out ....

He was very glad to stop paddling. His arms were now pretty sore, his legs were sunburnt, his stomach was just a little tired of bananas and his nose was the colour of a drunken setting sun. One lesson, however, he had learnt. The jungle, at first sight, looked homogenous. On closer inspection, however, like the moods of the sea, it was always changing and yet each view in its own right was magnificent, the result of years.

He embarked. Thinking that the bursar's wife wanted to buy the piroque[17], he tied it alongside the boat before the latter sailed. This was a much smaller version of the Kisangani to Kinshasa ferry; again there was one bit with the engine pushing a large barge for second class passengers and stores. Towards the end of the first day, the ship ran aground. In attempting a reflotation, the front bit was released; after drifting somewhat precariously, it dropped an anchor. And then, Baha's piroque[17] saved the day. He was asked to paddle over to the parent ship which would use it to carry out some depth sounding trials downstream.

As mentioned earlier, the Zairois liked to propel their canoes from a standing position. Baha, sitting in the back with his two paddles, amused them somewhat. Then they took command and, while he was being entertained and fed with some rather special bananas by the Captain, they in turn amused him. To stand in this canoe was nigh on impossible – he now realised how useless this 'S' - shaped piroque[17] was. But to sit in the stern and paddle from there was, to them, distinctly alien if not also impossible. Eventually, after several manoeuvres usually associated with ducklings, they succeeded. Off they went. After a successful recce, Baha returned to his own second class barge, only to find that his prospective buyer had cried off.

The next morning, the ship refloated. Because of the shallow waters, only day-time travel was possible. At night, the ship would run itself aground on some suitable sandbank. By day, with two men at each bow rotating long sticks for depth-soundings, each one in turn singing out the depth, the journey continued with only one **more grounding. Again, like the larger ferry, this boat had its small** share of animals; this included turtles and two crocodiles. They were alive but, at only about five feet (1.5 m) long, fairly young. Like humiliated dunces, their forelegs were tied behind their backs, and their mouths were bandaged shut. Stationery, lying with their stomachs on the hot tin deck, they patiently awaited their unknown fate, their two large globular eyes scanning through three hundred and sixty degrees at all elevations looking for sympathy or solace. Little was received. There was nothing they could do .... except .... a tear.

Crocodiles were hunted by night. From a piroque[17], a light was held high and this would lure the animals forward. The two eyes, **reflecting the light like those of a cat, would be clearly visible. When the range closed, the animal was speared;** its defence lay in its backlash, which could easily result in the canoe's capsize, the crew's death by drowning and their eventual consumption by a victorious crocodile when it felt they had rotted to a delicate, stinking adequacy.

There were, of course, fellow passengers. During one conversation, while munching some raw peppers, Zairois 'authenticité' (a policy of general indigenisation) was discussed. This particular fellow had accepted certain western ideas and innovations, like internal combustion engines, long trousers, beer and Christianity (western? .... well, westernised). But his President had called for authenticity. Obedient to the far from bitter end, he had bought himself, for the tolerably fair price of £150, a second wife. This, apparently, did not clash with his Christian ideas. What the President says, goes. Authenticité!

In many countries, brides were still bought. Assets like good looking and hard working still counted while education had inflated the price a little. Some Africans were polygamous, many now were not, most Christians definitely not. Rare indeed, however, in days gone by, had been the spinster, bachelor or prostitute. Their society had not allowed such. Only one thing was scorned - sterility, invariably blamed on the woman. To many Africans, and to his

99

mother, Baha, a thirty year old bachelor with but a bicycle for company, was quite incorrigible.

They reached Mbandaka, on the more substantial river Zaire. All disembarked. Now the Kinshasa ferry was not due for another week or so. Indeed, nothing was going down-river for about ten days. This, for visa reasons if nothing else, was not good. So he bought food and relaunched himself in the unwanted 'S'-shaped piroque[17]. A little crowd of children and passers-by, amused rather by this unusual spectacle, wished him well with a very loud and cheerful "au revoir". Now he had no intention of paddling all the way to Kinshasa; what he hoped to do was to find a small trading boat and to tie up with him. Hitch hikers are always better off on the road; Baha went on the river. It was, however, so wide that the first barge to overtake him, the only one that day, was well out of ear shot, despite a valiant, long paddle towards. He continued his drifting and reading, trying not to be too engrossed in his latest book, a new and much more captivating story by a Russian author. His bog book now served just the one purpose.

He was later to regret missing that lift. Towards the end of the day, while paddling happily towards the sun, a fisherman asked if he would like to spend the night with him. It was a little early but he felt it was silly to refuse an invitation. So they aimed for his small village, a collection of just half a dozen huts, small wicker jobs on stilts, by the water's edge. Soon, another piroque[17] came to escort him, and the first one disappeared. Then, in the village, no-one seemed to want to converse, although they knew French.

'Odd,' thought Baha. He looked for his book. Before dark, the first fisherman returned but he too was silent. Again, Baha considered this behaviour peculiar, but he didn't wonder why.

Soon, comparative peace was superseded by a confused atmosphere, not a little tense. It was now dark. A piroque[17] with an outboard arrived. One chap approached the village elder while another started manhandling the bike. Baha went to intervene, initially verbally and then physically. In the subsequent small maul, Baha gave up; after all, one of them had a knife and both were drunk. He was pushed, shoved and forced into the outboard. His belongings were thrown in on top and off they went to the other side of the broad river. It was more than a little worrying. All was without a word of explanation. Thoughts and imaginings passed, with the noise of the outboard, into the expansive silence of the night.

There, on landing, stood the chief, ministered by many, ready to greet or eat, as instructed. Baha, the prisoner, was led up to him and sat down. All the villagers came to look at him as if he was some heinious martian, while the first fisherman explained everything to the chief. He spoke in his tribal language but, by the movement of the hands, Baha soon discovered what his twofold crime was: sitting, not standing, in his dug-out while using two, not one, paddles, with intent; secondly, he was a mzungu[10]. Eventually, the diatribe finished. There were cries of 'authenticité' and 'oyee'* which meant, as far as Baha could work out, that the case for the prosecution was therefore immediately valid and foolproof. A hundred years ago, he, the white man, would surely have been for the boiling pot. Now, his fate was obviously more civilised and more undecided, even if unbureaucratically so. Eventually, after many a good shauri[7], he was taken back to the other side and deposited in the original village. He had been pardoned. In the morning, he would be able to proceed. His host disliked the verdict.

That night, for other reasons, was dreadful. He was offered a little bed in a hut but his flimsy mosquito net was completely inadequate, as were, again, trousers and repellants. There was

* that same current Zairois political slogan with its rallying cry of an answer.

only one thing to do: sit in the smoke of the fire and keep on spraying the top half of the body with repellant. The mosquitoes would then settle for the trousers where they were more readily killed. He read; book in one hand, torch in the other. There were many interruptions while he aimed yet more death blows. His trousers soon became covered in little blood spots. Despite tiredness and further attempts at going to bed, he didn't sleep at all. The same, to a certain extent, happened to one old boy who also sat by the fire armed with a long cloth. Perhaps one shouldn't condemn the Africans, therefore, when they, like the mosquitoes, sleep by day.

Baha resolved to leave at first light, mainly to avoid further ill-treatment. It took a long time to come but then, after only one extra small shauri[7], he was off.

"Do you like tourists?" he asked in farewell. Silence remained. The sun rose behind him. He was mighty glad to be free again. But after paddling only a couple of miles, he heard the dreaded noise of that blasted outboard again. He was re-arrested. He cursed. At least they were now sober, but this meant no increase in their sense of logic or justice.

They were taking him to Mbandaka. "Why?" he asked. Because they were taking him to Mbandaka. He fell silent. They were taking him .... but not directly of course. En route, they stopped for the odd chat with a cousin or two, and these existed in Gilbertian proportions. At ten, they stopped in a small town - the rest of the journey was apparently to be by bus. Were there any buses? The rest of the journey was to be by lorry. Were there ....? Baha was beginning to run out of patience. Fortunately, however, they met the local 'chef' and he persuaded everybody that Baha and all were well.

'And that was the end of that' thought he. He was wrong. They demanded money to pay for the petrol! What a sense of humour! But no, they were serious. He, helpless, gave them some and the chef helped too. They started drinking. He sat to wait. It appeared that, because they were black and he was not, they could do anything to him without fear of recrimination. God, he wanted to get away. The chef consoled him with a beer. Then, out in the river, he saw a small trader. He asked, and one chap interrupted his alcoholic intake to take him out and embark him on this barge. And this fellow, still tolerably sober, spoke of undying friendship - Baha just couldn't understand his innocent gall. Onboard, the ship's captain welcomed him. At last, peace and safety.

Looking back, to have had only this one occasion of open hostility in seven months was pretty good. Would a lonely African travelling in Europe have fared so well?

This small barge, a veritable phut-phut, took him to Kinshasa. Again stops were made by night whence mosquitoes - numerous, tedious and odious beasts - returned to the attack. Everyone sat patiently, flicking themselves with rags until either tiredness or the dawn created a diversion. In these jungle areas, there were really only ten minutes of the day which were heavenly: five at dawn and the rest at dusk. It was then cool and quiet, the mosquitoes or flies had gone and the flies or mosquitoes hadn't yet come. Three pleasant days (flies are few in midstream) and two ghastly nights later, when the river passed from dense jungle to open, hilly country, the mosquitoes disappeared. Because of them and because of navigational difficulties in the jungle areas - difficulties due to the river being so wide; islands, small and large, being so numerous; the line between river and land, on account of the many swamps, being so indiscernible; and the height of a canoeist's eye being measured in only inches - it was probably just as well that he went by barge. On one afternoon, an odd phenomenum took place. Above were thin clouds; through these, diffraction occured, and gorgeous shades of blues and greens were overhead.

Lavatorial problems were more easily solved aboard this trader. Such, in the piroque[17], necessitated occasional stops and steps into the jungle - two of the latter were usually sufficient for total decency. On this barge, though, was one of the earlier versions of the thunderbox, loosely connected to the stern. It was made of thin aluminium sheeting held together by some random iron supports. When the barge was stationary, a visit there, as in a waiting railway train, was a shade anti-social. And when the barge was at its only other speed - full ahead - the entire structure shook in sympathy with the main engine and in antipathy of its user. Inside this resonating chamber, with one's feet on the two metal strips called a floor, and with the turbulent wake providing a continual and automatic flush, one could barely manage a successful george let alone a quiet perusal of the stock market.

Just before reaching Kinshasa, nearly everybody on board went up for'ard and, led ably by an old man who up until then had

103

been constantly reading his bible, danced, and danced hard and fast, shaking fists, heads and hips at the port beam. Ten minutes later, sweating profusely, they returned. Apparently, this was done to pacify some weird creature, a Neptune or a Loch Ness Monster.

It was a joy to return to Kinshasa, to shave in a mirror, to sit on a loo, to eat something other than cassava; his hostess, looking after him for the second time, bless her, didn't like cassava either. A sample of this he had bought for her in the market. Despite several visits there, and a large cosmopolitan population in the city, he never saw another mzungu[10] amongst the crowded stalls. But he did find one old mama, sitting behind her few wares on the pavement, who spoke Swahili.

"Jambo[2] mama." They were off; both exceedingly happy.

Only a day or two could he spend relaxing, listening to music, reading home newspapers, and basking by a swimming pool while casting on idle ear to a neighbour's radio which reported that Liverpool were well on the way to winning the cup. There was time too to go to church, though the only way to get a service in English was to attend a rather American performance. Alleluia in a yankee accent doesn't sound so joyful somehow, but no doubt it is received with equal enthusiasm at the other end.

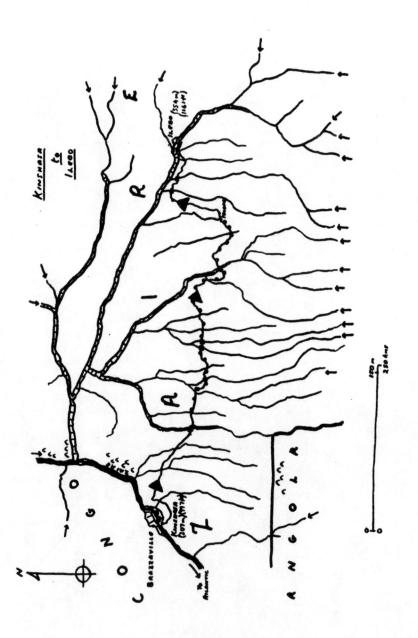

Chapter 8.

ICE-CREAM.

He had five days in which to get to Lubumbashi and the Zambian border, a distance, as the crow flies, of almost a thousand miles (1600 km). Quite a crow. He thought he would cycle to start off with as it was a fairly good road which led out of Kinshasa (the second and only other road out; he had taken the first one, the one to the west, after his January visit). An overnight stop re-introduced him to cassava and mosquitoes .... and African spinach which was quite nice. After two days and just before the roads got bad, he paused to await a ferry. Here, delays were frequent and long, and traders did well. With his own cassava and dried fish, he sat by the riverside to dine. Eyes and conversation turned to this non-cheese-and-wine-hamper-eating mzungu[10]. Later, on the road once more, just as the rains began to fall, a lorry passed, recognised him and stopped. He accepted a lift; perhaps that was the wrong word. On these surfaces, one had to hang on for one's very life - his only loss was a bit of his one remaining front tooth. At other times, the lorry got firmly stuck and it took everyone working with spades, shrubbery and muscles to get it loose again. He travelled in a succession of lorries over vast open rolling plains which separated many river valleys. These, in contrast, were densely wooded. The rivers, all northbound tributaries of the river Zaire, were invariably crossed by ferry. Along the banks lived a few fishermen, on the plains were occasional villages but usually the lands were empty. One exception was a field full of women collecting caterpillars. In some fields, alas, all vegetation had been burnt - more needless destruction. Vast areas remained void and virgin, awaiting the advent of man and his agriculture, or perhaps man will make a game park though visitors from Longleat might scorn such artificiality. Animals were reported to exist, but none were seen.

On one lorry, while trying to rescue his foot from underneath a grandmother, (the lorries were invariably pretty packed for there were no buses along these routes), he went through what was by now a routine. Try Swahili*, then French, then brute force. The lorry

---

* Swahili was one of Zaire's four national languages. All are Bantu[16] tongues and, to a limited extent, similar. At this stage, Baha was soon to re-enter Swahiliphone Africa.

owner, 'le patron', on hearing that Baha spoke Swahili, invited him into the driver's cab for a chat. From henceforth he was treated royally, being offered both food and drink. During one meal, more 'authenticité', this time on a friendly note, was seen. The lunch consisted of palm wine, ("Oyee!"), cassava, ("Oyee!"), and, er ...., a tin of Japanese fish, (oh dear.) Before parting after a night of soporific splendour on top of beer bottles, Baha tried to work out how much to tip 'le patron'. He got two notes (about £2) ready. Instead, he was given money. Refusal was refused. Fantastic kindness.

At Idiofa, he ran out of lorries. The road however was now better so, still in a hurry, he continued 'by-de-bike'. On top of the plains were good views. Yet again, there was a superb tropical sunset; his elongated shadow danced back and forth in the thick, long and now golden grass. Grass? - it was at least head high. He was contemplating a camp for the night when a lorry came and took him for a few miles before depositing him, with two others, at a junction. The three walked into the night, one into a snake. The immediate reaction was to kill. With Baha's cycle, they trapped its head and mercilessly attemped to break its neck and windpipe by repeated pressure on the wheel. It wriggled, shook in pain. Animals, though, are rather tougher than humans; it took advantage of a small mistake and slithered quickly into the bush. Gone. All slept at a collectivité.

After a further day and a half on the bike, during which, for the first time, he had a physical ailment which impeded his cycling, a swollen ankle, he reached Ilebo to discover the train had left the previous day. Twice, he had become even more convinced of the usefulness of the bicycle. At one stage, they doubled the price of petrol. And then, just before Ilebo, he had come to a river crossing where quite a few lorries were waiting.

"The ferry broke down three days ago," they explained. Yet again the bike travelled by piroque but this one was only hired, not bought. Much cheaper. A three day wait preceded the train journey to Lubumbashi. He waited impatiently, for his continued presence in Zaire was now illegal, staying at the local mission with another lonesome traveller, an atheist whose only comprehensible belief in life was apparently that Christian missions should look after him free of charge. Perhaps he wasn't too wrong. Some missionaries live, by western standards modestly, but by African yardsticks, very

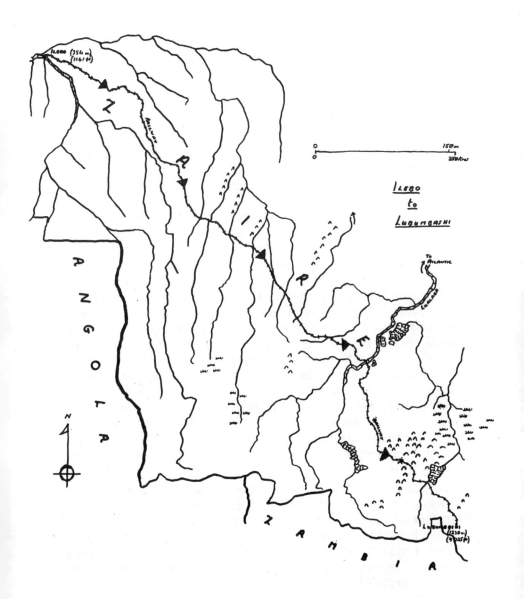

Ilebo (354 m)
(1161 ft)

Railway

Z
A
I
R
E

ANGOLA

N

ZAMBIA

150m

250km

ILEBO
to
LUBUMBASHI

To Atlantic

Lubilash

Railway

Lubumbashi (1230 m)
(4035 ft)

comfortably thank you. Levels entertained by the 'filthy-rich' tourist and big spenders generally remain, to the African, incomprehensible, and to an educated and compassionate world, inconsistent with modern ideas of conservation. There again, there are travellers who tour foreign lands on a shoestring although their eyes tell them how relatively rich they are. Students, possessing those cards which give them travel concessions in even the poorest of countries have, unwittingly perhaps, become when abroad a twentieth century priveleged class. (One hears that in some countries of the Middle East, these cards are forged and sold on the black market: and thus there is a form of third world corruption which depends almost entirely on a corrupt developed world for its existence. One for the psychadelic pot?) Meanwhile, Baha's visa had expired.

His wait was interrupted by a local wedding. A sea of colour was the congregation, though bride and groom looked a little artificial in their comparatively mundane and European black and white. Music was purely traditional, played as it was on drums, cymbols and an actual tom-tom; it was a cylinder of wood down which one line was cut, and via this the instrument was hollowed. For rythms, it was beaten with two small padded sticks and, sure enough, you (well they) could get different notes out of it. For the music alone, the service was worthwhile. There was, however, another great difference between an African and a European wedding: at times like this of such great joy, women present make a piercing trilling sound of no mean volume. Amongst those who watch, happiness beams from so many eyes. Meanwhile, the couple look sad. Indeed, not once during the service did they smile, nor would it have been right for them to do so. Such are their ways.

The train ride consisted of seventy two hours on wooden seats; the only thing modern about this journey was the ticket Baha received for his bike - a used computer card. The coaches were packed. Sometimes one couldn't even stretch a leg for there, under the seats, was a woman and her children sleeping on just a cotton cloth. Frequently, stores filled all available space and one became almost imprisoned. The worst of these were the sacks of dried cassava; everything and body was covered in a thin white dust. Baha's problems were not helped by his health. His ankle had swollen further and now the other one, the left one of course, was coming out in sympathy. Twice he treated himself to a beer in the comfort of the second class restaurant car.

"Why don't you travel second class and get a sleeper?" a Zairois asked.

"I prefer to meet the simple folk, to see their traditional foods and customs." Admittedly there were not many of the latter in a third class railway carriage, but the inference, that his questioner was to a certain extent Europeanised, was not too well received. He, a nouveau riche Zairois, was immediately recognised as such by the presence of a beer paunch. Elsewhere in the country, the menfolk, farmers and fishermen, were fit and well built. Their stomachs were concave; there was not a surplus ounce anywhere. Their women in comparison were large and buxom, but not without beauty or for that matter strength. Wealth seemed to reverse the balance, men putting on, as it were, what women take off.

Talking of clothes, womenfolk were always smart. The general trend was to wear a two-piece costume, a close fitting blouse which accentuated the waist and a long flowing skirt. A further length of material was for holding the baby on the back, while any luggage was balanced on the head. These skirts were invariably gaily coloured and often rather personal. Positioned, inevitably across the expansive buttocks, was a picture of an important dignitary, usually, but not always, the President. Sometimes he looked at you from a small bottom; sometimes from a broader base; but Presidents were definitely in. (Coups d'état tend to disrupt more than just governments.) Where the custom originated was difficult to tell but two bums gave Baha an idea or two; one V.I.P., set against a background of spitfires, soldiers and submarines, was Sir Winston Churchill; another recalled our Golden Jubilee of 1937.

Hairstyles also varied enormously. Some were platted into furrows, others twisted into long spokes jutting from the head in all directions, and on these two basic themes existed many unique creations. The men, more modest on the head, were often equally flamboyant in the shirt. This, in gay colours, again reminded all of the President, of his revolution or of his political party, but not of his bank account.

At Lubumbashi, he left the train and aimed for the border. A few passengers made their exit prematurely, some hundreds of yards before the train stopped in the station. They threw out their sacks of cassava and baggage, and then themselves before rushing to reclaim possession. The strong presence of police in the station

111

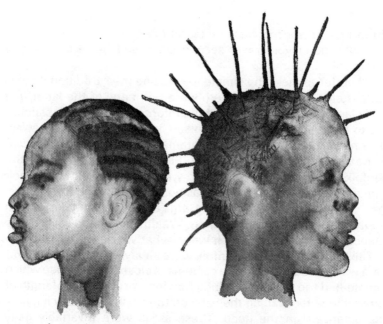

was perhaps the reason for this pre-emptive exodus. Having got through the officialdom, Baha wished to take off his long trousers and put on shorts. At what he thought was a quiet spot, having bought some food, he attempted the change. But it was difficult. A few of the women followed him, intent on a revelation. Later, in shorts and out of town, he took a wrong turning. He was soon surprised by a border post. He entered Zambia. By so doing here, he was probably rather lucky - at the only other but bigger immigration check point, questions about his protracted and thus illegal presence would almost certainly have been asked.

He travelled on the dirt road to Solwezi. By now his ankles were not too bad under bandages. What the ailment was, or why it went down again, he never learnt. While it was still early morning, he went a short way into the forest for a george. Much care was needed. In every direction he saw spiders' webs which, with the dew still on them, glistened as on a frosty morn. In the middle of each was one of those black and gold spiders, a good three to four inches (8 to 10 cms) long. All slept.

And later he stopped for a roadside pee. Just as he was finishing, he heard clapping from an old man standing behind him. Baha, to put it mildly, was puzzled. It was, he learnt with relief,

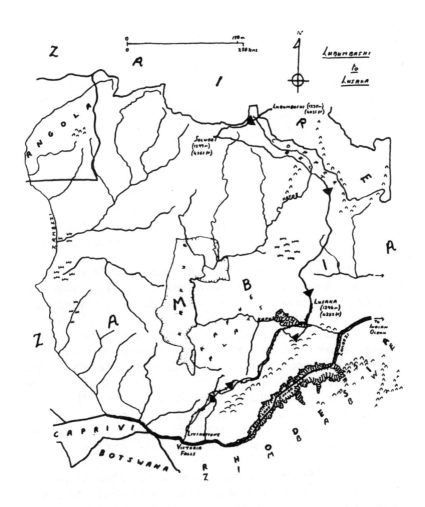

having first checked his flies, just a traditional form of greeting to which he clapped in return. Along this road were hundreds of butterflies of all colours and sizes, some very beautiful. It was not obvious that human neighbours practiced apartheid.

From Solwezi, down through the copperbelt and on to Lusaka, life was very different. The country side was rather flat, the road was excellent and his diet touched unprecedented luxury; fresh milk, eggs, ice-cream, everything was available. The horizons of poor old Stanley and Livingstone, Baha thought, had never revealed ice-cream fountains, but there again, they hadn't seen immigration posts either. He found it difficult to obtain mealie meal even in towns, though this, when compared to the cassava of Zaire, was bliss. In traditional settlements, it was of course there. In one, four schoolboys entertained Baha royally; in another, tribal ways were maintained even though the village was but seven years old. Its chief, for the sake of progress, had uprooted everything in order to come and live near the main road. Among much sophistication, there were still many wide open spaces of virgin bush; he saw little wild life - just hundreds of large and ugly cantilevered insects which seemed to enjoy warming themselves on the tarmac prior to being run over.

The roads were not busy; just the occasional fellow went by. One didn't, indeed couldn't. Here Baha was able to repay some inter-cyclist hospitality - it was long overdue. This particular chap had a puncture, and Baha had by now done enough of these to turn a string vest into an anorak. Close inspection revealed a tube looking poorer and older and distinctly more perforated than its octogenarian owner; he alas had run out of spare parts, puncture outfits and luck. Previous punctures had been repaired, not with a patch, but with a piece of string! The offending hole had been exiled by tying the adjacent rubber tightly together, as one does with a balloon. This particular tube had three or four such knots - what rubber remained was stretched, like the more feminine varieties, to the limit.

At night, life often held a little surprise. When stopping in a village, his passport was first asked for. After all and sundry had read it, it was passed to the chief who would then decide whether or not the visitor was a bona fide tourist. If his decision was yes - Baha never received a no - all would welcome him. But this initial reception left a slight chill. The nights were definitely cold. It was

114

now May, Zambia's winter. In his tent and sleeping bag, he had to wear everything he possessed in order to keep warm. And in the mornings, he had to wear his anorak, especially if the road was downhill, until the sun had warmed the air. 'Twas fresh and crisp. A steep descent made one feel rather like a tube of toothpaste.

Before leaving Nairobi, a friend had given him the address of a bird in Lusaka and she, by letter, had agreed to look after him. After a long time on the road, he knocked on her door a little apprehensively. A blonde. She told him his friend had just married another bird. What finer friend. Yet even she, Baha left behind in order to go to Livingstone, to see the falls and to stay with a vicar!

The road from Lusaka first passed over the Kafue river before rising into the hills. From there, the view backwards, over the valley, was memorable. From the other side of these hills, he looked over the Kafue Flats, a veritable sea of land. It stretched for miles and miles before disappearing, because of the sheer distance, in a haze. The miles ticked slowly by.

Tick.

One's first impression of Victoria Falls was that of a rural Euston station in the days of steam - days that, alas, are no more, except in the House of Commons. There, ahead of one, was a mighty cloud rising out of the earth and from under it came a constant roar. The falls at this time were magnificent; it was the slump of the tourist season and the end of the rainy one (by pure luck, Baha was invariably in a country during its dry season, the one exception being when he was in southern Zaire, and happily en train). One could sit for hours just watching the great volumes of water cascading downwards, the clouds of spray leaping upwards, and the brilliantly clear rainbows which the bright sunlight produced therein. It was a superb spot for idle thoughts - he lacked a lass - a pity he had left that bird in Lusaka.

One was able to climb out onto an island just in front of the falls. There, the wind currents were strong and confused and, because of the spray in which they blew, damp indeed. One was soon soaked. But it was well worth it. In such conditions of warmth and humidity, vegetation flourished. Up top on the banks were the dry and open plains; here in the gorges was an instant tropical jungle. A little further downstream, one could climb right down to the water's edge at a spot appropriately called the boiling point. The raging waters forced their way through the gorge and under the railway bridge. There, the monkeys were ignoring the border closure, as was the odd railway wagon which one Rhodesian engine would push on and deposit while another, from the Zambian side and at a much later hour, would come and discreetly collect. But those monkeys were everywhere; one, picking hairs as usual, came within a yard or two.

At breakfast the next morning with the vicar, they remarked to each other,

"Oh don't worry. This is Africa. There's no hurry. The train is bound to be late." Baha arrived at eight o'clock exactly, only to see the eight o'clock train pulling out of the station. Moral? So he spent another day at the falls where, as at the guardrail of a ship at sea, it was possible to spend hours in peaceful solitude (as long as you could forget that just behind you there was one of those modern, formica-tipped, tourist hotels). He decided to cycle up 'riverside drive'. On his left, where they should be, namely at a distance and in the water, were some hippos bathing. On his right, behind a game park fence, was the odd gazelle. In front of him, the road

118

twisted along the picturesque river bank until, round the corner, he suddenly saw an elephant. Both stopped, the one riding, the other eating. It looked tame enough but proof was not required. Baha turned round.

And instead, he went to look at the gorges, formed by years and years of the falls gradually walking backwards up the river in a zig-zag manner. There were some tremendous views from the tops of vertical cliffs overlooking the still turbulent waters a few hundred feet below. The occasional buck surprised him, as did something that looked like an uncommercial bushbaby.

"More toast?" asked the vicar at the next morning's breakfast.

"I'd better go." With half an hour to spare, he was in the station. The train left two hours late and arrived in Lusaka after a journey which should have taken about twelve hours but which actually lasted for twenty four. Moral? Some stories have no morals. Further puzzlement was caused by the price paid for carrying the bicycle - twice as much as his own fare.

Back to the bird. But, at Baha's request, I shall talk only about Lusaka, a very 'Europeanised' city except for much metallic banging as pots and pans were assembled in the spotlessly clean market place. It was a rare sight, in an African market unless it was a Zambian one, to see everything wrapped up in polythene. At last, flies were few. A further distinctive feature in Zambia was noticed - many babies wore nappies; in other and more rural parts of Africa, the cheapest and most hygenic post-natal underwear was usually fresh air.

This time, when he left, he aimed for the expanses to the East and then Malawi. This road was a bit more African; no longer was it possible to feed on ice-creams, and mealie meal was more readily available. The road, after some miles over more flats, rose into the hills through which the river Luangwa forces its way to the Zambezi. How it decided to chose a route through this mass of hills was puzzling - initially it must have stopped in lakes for a think. The river's bridge was quite impressive though again, when stopping for the night, Baha was often questioned. Chaps were a little worried that the bridge was to be blown up by some terrorist for a second time.

On his first night out, however, there were no questions. On stopping for a chai[5], one or two Africans started to make general rhubarb noises, similar to descriptions of Chelsea by Leeds

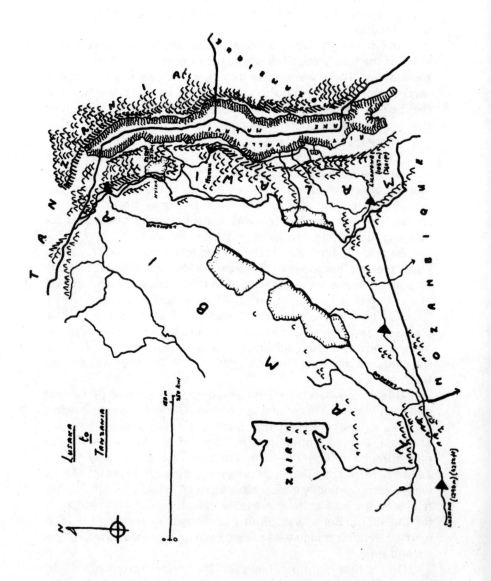

120

supporters, in their tribal language. As usual on such occasions, Baha added some remarks in Swahili. As soon as they realised that this mzungu[10] had bothered to learn an African tongue, ableit only partially, the rhubarb usually stopped. This time, the result was more - a Swahili speaker invited him home for the night. Unfortunately, however, the evening was not very pleasant - he was a rather drunken schoolmaster who spent the entire time with his mouth full of either beer or words; the latter, derogatory in the extreme, concerned his drunken headmaster. Most of the comments, equally applicable to himself, were true. Part of the evening was spent in a bar through which most people passed. On bidding farewell, the headmaster said,

"Make sure our fine guest has at least one good woman tonight." Outside, he was introduced to one, a comfortable wench. But Baha declined, not only because of the concrete floor which was his bed.

Baha spent the second night at a mission, though here too the initial reception was rather cool. The first one to see him, admittedly it was a shade dark, rushed to tell the padre of the presence of a cyclist armed with spears - the very devil on wheels. He learnt about tent poles, and Baha learnt of the sweet taste of a well cooked wild boar.

After some more steep and varied hills covered in lonely bush forest, the land went flat again, but not completely uninteresting. Outside one petrol station he saw two bullocks waiting, with somewhat incorrigible looks on their faces, while their cart's loads, petrol drums, were filled. Transport modernisation was perhaps a little gradual. Later, when approaching the hills near the border, Baha met a fellow cyclist with whom he started chatting. He was a 25-year old in his last year at primary school - for the third time. (In Central Africa, this was not unusual.) He invited Baha to spend the night, explaining that his home was just a few miles ahead. Fortunately, there was a full moon, for his estimation of distance was well over 100% out. This was rather a common failing, perhaps associated with their virtue of patience. Their sense of direction remained true.

That night, after a meal of mealie meal and pumpkin leaves eaten, as ever, with bare hands, they sat and discussed Zambia's social problems.

"Oh, our fault is that we are lazy," they said with remarkable

121

honesty, "and we have this stuff called 'seven days beer'. The women make it in five days and it's only good for two. You've got to drink fast. It's a pleasant habit, at only a fraction of the cost of the bottled products."

In a town just before the Malawi border, he found a café selling steak and chips. Too much. He was rapidly tiring of mealie meal. He ate two platefuls. Soon, it was back to the dust roads. And it was from dust to dust, for car after car went by, all imports for Zambia coming up from Blantyre.

In Lilongwe he was looked after by first a British couple, who thought he looked a bit helpless and took him in, and then a Dutch family who got him on the rebound. He was driven round - by car, what joy - the new capital city development where many a pound was being spent, perhaps aesthetically, perhaps recklessly, on modern parliament buildings, embassies and other bureacratic beauties. In the market, however, was Africa. And so was many a juicy mandarin orange.

On the Sunday, he headed north on a lonely road. He was in shamba[1] country again. The local houses were partially modernised and partially still traditional, as indeed they were in parts of eastern Zaire, though in a different style. Glass windows, doors and verandahs were built into a slightly bigger home in which the mud brick and straw thatch remained. After a night in the hills, where shelter had been granted to him only after a succession of interviews with grander and yet grander chiefs, he descended

slowly towards Lake Malawi, the first glimpses of which were seen from some thirty miles (48 km) away. He passed through a game reserve but, despite numerous warnings of elephant, he saw neither man not beast. By the side of the lake, for that was where the road now lay, he stayed for three days. He was told that, though he was lucky to meet no elephants in the game reserve, he could rest assured that the crocodiles were few and friendly. Smile please. And superb it was, when feeling a little hot, to stop for a swim. He camped twice on the beach, starting and finishing the days with more swims in those crystal clear waters. While the lake stayed on his right, the hills beyond in Mozambique, and those on his left, provided constantly changing scenery - a most pleasant alternative to the comparatively flat Zambia. Yet again, he was in Africa's rift valley. He ate some fish, caught, no doubt, by the nets of fishermen in their piroques[17] which were much more circular in cross section than those of Zaire.

As the silent hours passed with only insects to provide background song, the moon, the dawn, the sun and a Baha rose, all but the last over those distant hills to the East. Somehow, for real beauty at the rising of a celestial body, it seems that waters too are needed to make it thus. The still waters of this lake allowed many an early reflection to beam warmly. Rise further did Baha, on the hard road to Mzuzu. The rift valley was sometimes like a clean, knife-edge cut; elsewhere, it resembled more a compound fracture of hills and vales. Such was the case here. Gradually he climbed. From each ridge or hill-top he was able to look back for even more distant views of the lake. Hills which initially looked large were soon dwarfed by perspective and amongst them, as ever, sat little homes in their shambas[1]. What price the twentieth century when such, with a few medecines and education, was available. So too were many black monkeys and, in one chai[5] dukah[4], pure white rats. Contacts with locals varied; Swahili was a passport to free bananas, while the bicycle ensured two chats with canvassing M.P.'s, recognisable by brief cases and large lapel badges.

By the end of the day he was some three thousand feet (900 m) higher, and tired. In the morning life was easier for he was now on a plateau surrounded by, like the ridged icing on a birthday cake, a rim of hills. As he progressed northwards, the hills closed until at the end the road squeezed through a small pass before heading out west. Then it started climbing again onto another, higher plateau,

123

the Nyika game park. The road, already rough, became steep. He pushed, a lot. As the hours went by, he hoped the miles would also. He asked a lonely workman how far he had come.

"Fourteen miles."

"Nonsense!" said Baha, convinced he had come further, convinced that here was another African with a useless sense of distance. Around the next corner stood a milestone....

Soon, or rather not quite so, he had climbed a further 3000 feet (900 m) and the road, at last, was flatter; he was on top. On the two day trip from Mzuzu he had seen little apart from locust-type insects which, on taking off, revealed brilliant scarlets and mauves - rather like, as part of their service, the ladies of Wimbledon. Now, as he approached the game park entrance, he saw the first signs thereof, a few buck.

At the gate, he expected some formalities.

"Oh no," replied the warden, "only cars have to be out before sunset because they can sometimes kill animals which get mesmerised in their headlights. But you can stay throughout. I mean, after all, who has ever heard of animals being killed by a cyclist."

Baha was more worried by the opposite, having heard of the presence of lions and buffalo. He saw, however, only a few eland, some duikah, a surprised game warden fellow cyclist, and a rest house keeper who told him to go away. The main beauty in the park were the views. To the east were great, gently undulating, grassy plains with the occasional clump of trees; to the west, from the plateau's edge, rolling hills of a more rugged and forbidding nature oscillated to the horizon. Soon he was heading down into a rich, green valley, the view from its head was magnificent. The road spiralled to descend - he was walking again, straining to stop the loaded bike going too fast. A small waterfall cascaded downwards. The golden rays of the setting sun made the red earth look rich indeed. At the bottom of this steep hill lay the exit gate and rest for the night; he was entertained to mealie meal and lake fish - small jobs like sprats which his Lusaka bird had used as cat food.

The hills over which, the previous day, the sun had set, he now rode over, though on the more northerly legs, the road stayed in the valleys. Again, there were many splendid views, but these failed to console his stomach. A lunch of two soft drinks (yes, that wretched stuff is world-wide) was inadequate and by afternoon, the pangs of hunger were getting noisier. A woman was surprised but relieved to be able, on her lonely trek home, to sell some of her sweet potatoes. By night fall, just, he reached a town which rested under a great brown massif, over which only gazelle and a border could run. It was time for his day of rest and there, in the town, was a rest house. Having a bit of Malawi currency to get rid of, he partook of the luxury, thereby shattering one of his journey's principles, therein eating more mealie meal.

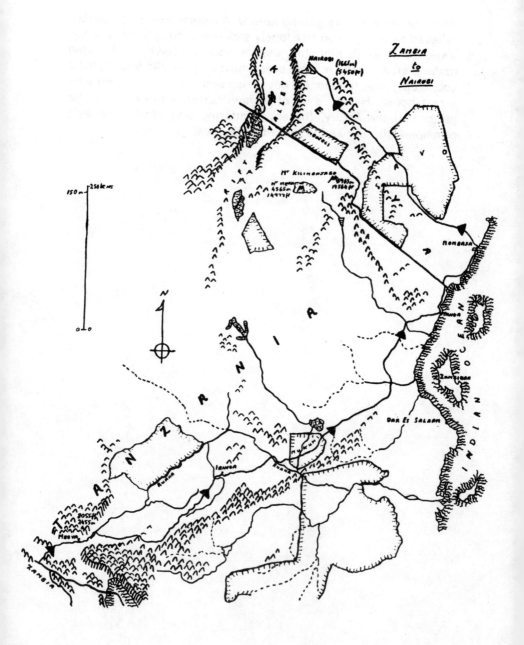

Zambia
to
Nairobi

NAIROBI (1665m)
(5450ft)

Mt KILIMANJARO
4565m
14977ft

MOMBASA

ZANZIBAR

DAR ES SALAAM

IRINGA

150m   250 kms

126

Chapter 9.

ENOUGH.

He now had that 'I'm nearly home' feeling. His money was running out, he was down to his last spare tyre (no more of this type were available in anglophone Africa), and he was beginning to think that he had had a none too elegant sufficiency. He left the rest house and, after only a few miles, the hills were all behind him. He was on the flats - Zambia again. At the border, he saw some Malawian court messengers; splendid relics of the British raj they were too, wearing army boots, gayters, baggy shorts, topees and a healthy dose of pride.

It was definitely Zambia by evening time; yet again a great red ball of a sun descended into a large haze, the fog of distance, which covered a dead and flat horizon.

Tanzania, initially, was hilly. He had to get across that old rift valley again and this involved the two sets of hills which enclosed it. At times, it was a little confusing as it seemed as if, south of Mbeya, he was in a great bowl. The town itself sat to the north amidst high and fertile lands. Here were signs indeed that someday the wide open spaces that are Africa may one day have, after cultivation and irrigation, a look not dissimilar from that of Norfolk (on an exceptionally clear day). As long as land remains agricultural, whether virginally, marginally or totally, it will retain its beauty. Baha, thinking he deserved a meal of European food, pitched his tent in a wee camp site. He was introduced to the askaris[13], three large dogs, which believed in either personal protection or warmth. They tried to share his tent, and one even took a fancy to his sleeping bag.

To the north of Mbeya, the rift valley fans out. On either side of the plains were the two lines of hills, and Baha's road stuck close to the right hand one. The view over these seemingly endless plains was magnificent - just the sheer expanse of it had beauty .... one wonders how glorious infinity will be. Back to earth, and the road descended but, every so often, it rose just a little for another glimpse northwards. Now, the agriculture was once more of the shamba[1] type, and in one such farmstead, separated from the next by miles of forest, he dined on ugali[6] again. The remains were given

127

to the animals - dogs, goats, doves and a cat - and as far as he could see, they received no variety. It did seem to be a most useful foodstuff. That that which eats it, the goat or the dove, tastes so much better is surely one of the mysteries and blessings of African life. Also for supper, but for the humans only, was, literally straight from the cow though both were a little shaken, milk. The cat, like any other animal, drank water - and why not?

Here the children were called by names not only Christian but also African, like Samweli rather than Samuel; those names limited by some ancient and Irish imagination, Patrick and Charles for example, were becoming less popular. The offspring, as ever, were tolerably numerous and pretty independent when it came to amusing themselves. In Britain, lads sometimes have wire-guided model aircraft. In Africa, such luxury is not found. One lad, however, had the answer. His pet was a large and ugly beetle which was duly fed and looked after and which, but for a small thread attached to one of its six legs, was free. When the time came for play, it was hurled skywards. Understandably, it became agitated, and flapped its wings in protest. Motion resulted. The lead tightened. Round it went. Only one thing was lacking .... a 'VRRRRM'.

A further day and night brought Baha to Iringa which sits on its own plateau at the head of a valley some thirty miles (48 km) long—a truly commanding position. Beyond, the road descended, first, gently so. To his right was a small monument which depicted the defeat of the Germans by the Wahehe people. Seeking culture and education, he went to read the plaque. It was in German. He returned to the road, a brand new, very smooth tarmac. His tyres made what to him sounded like a kissing noise.

'Not usually measured in r.p.m.' thought he in the small instant during which he remained in motion. Both tyres were punctured, thrice, by thistles.

'The price of culture.'

As evening approached, a further problem with the bike arose. He slowed to investigate. 'Twas a lonely part of the country though one or two huts were there. Looking at him were two women, sipping an evening beer; one, a landlady, smiled a big 'jambo[2]'. He slept in the 'pub'; and having drunk one beer, he could peacefully dream of the rest. In the morning, after a fabulous downhill stretch through green and virgin hills, he joined the river Ruaha. Over countless years, its waters had forged a path through many hills.

Their sides were often steep, their look rugged, their atmosphere eerie. As the river descended, it slowly swelled; its strength was manifest in the valley walls which grew in height as the seaward journey progressed. On the riverbanks stood a few green trees but elsewhere the vegetation looked lifeless. Great hulks of baobab stood silent. Between each tree or bush were large spaces of dry and dormant earth, soil sans soul.

The scene was set for rumours given to him at Iringa: that here were animals a plenty. But he only saw, among other things, a few snakes - one, ten feet (3 m) long and dying, wriggled painfully in its final agonies having been run over; another, four feet (1.2 m) long, which he accidentally hit but obviously did not injure; and yet a third, just a little smaller, which literally jumped into the air to get out of the way. The other things seen were some monkeys, fabulous views both up and down river, and articulated lorries. But amidst the loneliness of this silent, grey valley, these infrequent juggernauts brought what they can never carry - solace.

Later, the road parted from the river to climb up and over some hills, green and fertile once more, to Mukumi game park. As the main road went straight through this, he thought it would be fairly safe. Others thought otherwise; within half an hour he was offered six lifts. Before stopping to camp, he saw zebra, wildebeest, warthog, two distant hippos and a tolerably near elephant - all happily engaged with their own problems of survival.

He pitched his tent, watched by a herd of gazelle. In the evening, he met an 'old colonial' who spoke of animals which walked by night; of lions which slept on the warm tarmac road by day; of buffaloes which used tent-pegs as tooth-picks. He offered Baha the security of a hut for the night.

He slept well, but outside, his tent got wet. Next morning, while packing, more gazelle, wildebeest and warthog wandered nearby though, once on the road, life was fairly quiet. Apart from one large herd of impala he saw nothing, except for the odd car.

Until, when he was all alone again, on rounding a corner, he suddenly saw an elephant coming out of the bush. It was but forty yards away .... less. It was, by the size of its tusks, a lone bull. Its trunk, smelling man, was raised. Its mighty head was slowly nodding; it walked towards him with determination, its eyes firmly fixed on target, its large ears waving powerfully. Baha cycled as fast as he could. Worried glances over his right shoulder were made

without any reduction in speed. The distance apart grew larger. The elephant stopped. Only thus was the race won. He must have broken at least one all-comers' record.

He didn't feel safe again until some ten miles (16 km) later when he was out of the park and back among shambas[1] and people. In those ten miles he saw nothing else apart from monkeys and a bus transporting Chinese railway workers; they smiled in a somewhat revisionist manner.

That elephant encounter was the most dangerous incident of the trip. Again, he thought 'enough'. If it had been a lion, Baha could well have been accused of commercialisation, given the maker's name of his bicycle. He also wondered, much later when the danger no longer existed, whether or not that initial thought - 'It's a lone bull' - had been mutual.

He was pleased to spend a relaxing evening eating maandazi[12] and chatting idly.

"Oh I love the British climate," one Tanzanian said. "All that rain if not actual snow is wonderful - no insects!"

On another evening, when thinking of somewhere to sleep, he entered a small workshop in which some of the country's youth were engaged on a self-help project. He asked to camp. A few of the youths showed him to their leader who escorted him to the local chairman who led him to the police officer who directed him to a landlord who demanded seven shillings. At each stage he muttered,

"But I only want to put up my tent," though each subsequent protest was quieter than the former. By the time he had been shown a room, the rain had started. It later poured incessantly. He was glad indeed that his earlier protests had not been entertained. The rest house was definitely African: the room contained only a bed; the roof leaked; the loo was outside; the basin was a bucket; the booze was beer and the gramaphone needle was sorely scratched. A rainy day followed as did one further expenditure of seven bob for a similar no-star guest-house; his money was lasting nicely, his principles were weakening fast.

It was small shambas[1] and tiny villages from then on, though gradually the scenery and vegetation changed as he approached the Indian Ocean at Tanga. These villages, as others on Central Africa's main roads, tended to be somewhat modernised when compared with those more isolated. While some folk stood idle, others waited to sell in their dukahs[4] what few could afford, a few plied away at sewing machines, one or two competetively played record players while a luckier minority interested themselves in the sale or consumption of beer. In some centres, the market place was life's focus. There, invariably, a dukah[4] or two served food. And at Tanga, he entered the sea for something which resembled a swim but was in fact a bath.

Usually on this journey he had tried to vary his diet though about vitamins he knew nothing. Most dieticians try to change the food from meal to meal but, for the last few months, such had often been impossible. If, in one particular part of the country, he was only able to buy bananas, he would endeavour, on reaching a town, to buy something else. There was in any case, according to Baha, not a lot of point in making a meal nutritional if one couldn't spell it. Here in Tanzania, however, such was his passion, such also was the limited variety, that he ate maandazi[12] in town and country alike. With them, of course, came tea drunk from the saucer. In such hot climes, a cup takes a long time to cool.

But he could not slow down. In Tanzania, short shorts were likely, with their owner/occupier, to be arrested. This was understandable, even in a country where in the remoter areas one could meet women wearing beads and bangles round everything except their bosom which remained, in splendid isolation, naked.

131

His long trousers, despite two hurried patches put on in Iringa, were again wearing thin. He was a little sad to leave Tanzania for there his Swahili had definitely been useful. On initial meeting, some Tanzanians, especially the southerners, were a bit reticent; but once Swahili was mutually understood, they were friendly indeed, despite some misconceptions:

"Are you American or Chinese?" one asked.

After a few more miles of rough road, his trousers split .... just a few miles short of the Kenyan border. Although it was a coast road, he saw little of the sea. Instead he saw, afterwards, a large beetle which had just flown into him, a beast bigger than a big-toe with wings to boot. His only other in-flight collisions had been with flies; some had entered the eye to annoy, others had dived into the open and panting mouth and had reached the stomach before they had thought of Jonah or he of sauce. And he saw one large, hairy, sleeping tarantula .... almost fantastic .... there was, on consideration, no need of assistance in killing that swallowed fly.

At Mombasa, where the swaying palms give way to swinging cranes, he had a quick swim before starting on the last leg back to Nairobi. One worry remained, a worry accentuated by that elephant in Mukumi, and that was Tsavo game park which was renowned for its high population of elephants. On this his first day, however, the park was only on his right hand side and he was separated therefrom by a railway line. He saw little; just some monkeys, on his left, who were doing some human watching. Monkeys, for humans, were invariably in trees. Humans, for monkeys, were much more fascinating, coming on wheels - not normally two - and in all sorts of coloured skins which they were able to take off. Those light brown humans were the funniest for, on the rare occasions when they took off everything before sleeping in the sun, (an odd habit that one; all other animals seek the shade), one noticed they were not quite all brown. Just like we monkeys sometimes have bright red bums, they have some lily white ones.

The next day, when he was in the park proper, he saw the elephants, about thirty of which were within a hundred yards of the road. It was a hot day. They stood in small (if you see what I mean) groups in the measly shade of thorn trees, cooling their red and dusty selves with their large, fan-like ears. None moved. Baobab trees, barkless, branchless, dead or dying, wounded by so many thrusting tusks, reminded Baha that these animals were not always so tranquil.

He also saw, and had to stop and wait for, a large family of baboons which were crossing the road. Some darted straight across; others looked left, right, left again, right again .... they took rather a long time; yet others, ignoring highway and personal codes, sat down on the white line and scratched. A few sat to stare at Baha but quickly and understandably lost interest.

By lunchtime, he was out of the park. After another day and a half, in which he saw a few giraffe and waterbuck, he finished with just one further small incident. He stopped on a lonely road for a pee; like the proverbial breakfast cereal, a quick dik-dik shot out of the bush and headed for drier climes. The journey ended after seven months on a British export, and some 8000 miles (12,800 km) without pollution. During this time, he had not lost but rather gained a stone (6½ kg) in weight. Now, presumably, a time would follow during which muscle would turn to fat. He returned to Nairobi, a city with every amenity. He decided, after a good bath, to go out for a beer.

"I hope I don't get run over."

THE END

Appendix
CENTRAL AFRICA — AN IMPRESSION

The Present.

In the country, invariably sparsely populated, the people live in small huts or groups thereof. They work to survive, usually by subsistence agriculture, sometimes, as in the Zaire basin, by fishing. Their way of life, now unworried by tribal wars but blessed with a few twentieth century innovations, is rarely strenuous. Animals are free range. Fruit trees grow wild. The little boys do odd jobs while the girls — they have no need of toys — look after the plentiful babies. Everywhere, with the exception of some parts of Kenya and Nigeria, vast tracts of land await cultivation. They consist of hills or jungle or open rocky savannah, but only rarely, as in the sub-saharan areas, are they infertile. The potential is enormous. The limiting factors are rain, which is seasonal and often insufficient, and people. Men can, but seldom do, work hard. Boys sometimes act as shepherds. It is usually the women who do most of the work. If 'development' takes these women off the land before the men get on it, then some countries, the more industrialised Kenya and Zambia for instance, will have serious food problems.

The menfolk, by selling foodstuffs to the towns, are able to buy and enjoy a few modern items — beer, cigarettes, radios, clothes and some tinned foods. The nearer people live to the main road or river, the easier it is. The more successful become middle-men. But for food, the country, especially in the more right wing nations, would often stay completely undeveloped. Meanwhile the children, well some of them, go to school. Nearly all countries give a full primary education to most of their children. In the more Moslem areas of Nigeria and Cameroun (and perhaps C. A. R.) however, some fathers are not keen on western education. In other parts, financial reasons may limit schooling to just one or two offspring, invariably boys, from a family of perhaps eight or more. In school, sometimes painfully European (tunes like 'London bridge is falling down' are still heard), all kids learn about, among other things, towns.

Town life is certainly in the twentieth century. Modern parliament buildings, official residences, army barracks, international airports and housing estates are built, often with borrowed money. In them work a semi- if not complete elite — the educated African white collar worker. His wage is guaranteed. Like his European predecessors he can afford, on a more limited scale perhaps, sophisticated tastes. He probably has but one wife though a few have another up-country, about four kids per wife, and a beer paunch. (Poorer families, usually also monogamous, are invariably larger. The best form of birth control, as so often stated, is a higher standard of living; to achieve the former, aim for the latter. But Africa, except perhaps a few southern Nigerian cities, is not overpopulated.) Only in the towns will he, the African wage-earner, find modern homes, electricity, piped water, hospitals, properly equipped schools, fully stocked shops, modern entertainments and, oh dear, status.

Thus, people who can afford it prefer to live in towns. From these many others, small traders, taxi drivers and the like, make money. On these again live more. What there was has by now thinned out. Many town dwellers are poor; many are unemployed — these include the educated — and there is, there can be, no dole (it would cause a massive depopulation of the land). The poor, undoubtedly, would be better off in the country, where the cassava grows and the traditional ways of life guarantee a tolerable welfare to all despite age or illness. But if one stays in the country, one will never be rich. If one moves to the town, one can at least have hope though, to others, it is a thoroughly unrealistic one. To live in the city, even if only in the shanty towns thereof, is regarded as the "done thing'. Under the extended family system, one worker can find himself surrounded by numerous parasitical and idle relatives. It is ironic, but hardly surprising, that the richest most capitalist cities, Nairobi and Lagos, contain the poorest people and the worst slums, though both cities are working to better the conditions.

Cheap labour is exploitable. They work long hours for low wages. Some of the worst employers of African workers are their fellow Africans, though to expect instant social justice and effective trade unionism so soon is to be a little naive perhaps. As always, urbanisation is a source of many social ills.

It is in the towns, of course, that industries are based. Some countries have comparatively well developed, though rather localised, economic structures; there is oil in Nigeria, mining in Zambia and Zaire. Kenya has tourism. Other countries have to rely more heavily on agriculture. With foreign earnings and aid, further development is attempted. The more a country is agriculturally self-sufficient, the more development will be possible. Alas, few yet are. Funny: they were before independence, some old colonials point out; equally, they were self-sufficient before the white man arrived. Food imports in Central Africa are usually (though the rains are blamed) due to the faults of man.

Sometimes this word 'development' is applied to a multitude of sins. Amongst the prestige constructions are those more necessary for building up young nations. Police stations are needed, jumbo jets are not. Agricultural projects and import-substitution industries can make good sense. But money may be flittered away in excessively large armed forces, as in Zaire. Or perhaps the aid has strings — confer Chinese tomato juice in Tanzania; perhaps it is in effect administered by the donors — French corned beef and even French fresh carrots in Gabon; perhaps the recipient country is too closely aligned, albeit voluntarily, to its former colonial power — some Scandanavians suspect their aid to Kenya helps the ailing British economy. Aid however, is necessary, especially in the poorer areas like northern Zaire and C.A.R. It is sad, but very capitalistic, that most western aid goes to the richer lands, Kenya and southern Nigeria, where 'aid' brings in good returns. Elsewhere, aid donors seek raw materials. Gabon and Congo Brazzaville, it would appear, are being steadily raped of their trees in exchange for, in the former, a wrecked car in every village, and in the latter, many a bourgeois moped. Should one be surprised if some countries turn to the East? Congo Brazzaville

135

is trying. And, to quote a Tanzanian, "What does it matter if our stringy toothpaste is communist and not capitalist?"

Most political leaders, at the times of independence, spoke in socialist tones. They were times of ideals. But they inherited problems: the Mau-Mau for instance fought for Kikuyuland, but they were given Kenya, a country containing three basic ethnic groups and some sixty tribes. Of the latter, Nigeria and Tanzania each have over a hundred. Most countries are agreed, however, that their present national boundaries must remain. (A tribal division of Africa would have been dangerous and impossible.) All countries, no matter how many tribes are therein, have to build up a feeling of nationalism; it is necessary for development and progress; it is vital for political stability and peace. Expenditure on national prestige projects is thus understandable. (Political and sometimes personal ones should not be financed from similar sources.) Dictatorships, like those of Mobutu, deserve some praise if only because they have stopped civil wars. Other factors — inviolate leaders, strong armies, a censored press — should also be seen in this light of possible tribal conflict. Meanwhile, the religions of Christianity and Islam, materialism, education and industrialisation tend to lessen tribalism but it is a slow process. (And afterall, it took years before our Wars of the Roses were only recalled peacefully at annual cricket matches.) Already, in Nigeria, soldiers who fought each other are now serving in the same army. The vengeful tribalism will die, there is indeed hope.

Towards nationalist aspirations one often hears cries of 'Africanisation'. They usually infer that Europeans and/or Asians lose work permits. They sound racist. To a certain extent in Zaire they are, and in Uganda they definitely were. In Tanzania they are not. The results of Africanisation in most countries is that expatriates become fewer. Standards (western) of education (western) go down; industrial efficiency decreases; machinery breaks down, and civil service bureaucracy becomes a nightmare. But so what? Europeans in Europe are beginning to realise that productivity itself is not a cure-all. Africans know that they are not as good in these western tasks, but they do want to be themselves.

One advantage of a small — no country wants zero — expatriate population is that of the country's tastes. Many Europeans go to work in Africa for purely selfish reasons, and there is little wrong in that for one can't blame the donkey which eats its carrot; one can only blame the owner. While abroad, they still want to live like Europeans if not more so. Some expect all European foods and entertainments to be available. Because of lower standards of living and cheap local labour, some desire large houses and servants. Indeed in Kenya, where artificial fox scents are sometimes laid, the British can afford to be like the British of old while the British at home cannot. European tastes involve large imports, not least of which is oil. And such tastes mean that the aspirations of the local Africans, especially the young, are strongly affected.

To have an agriculturally based economy, which all countries want, one needs people on the land. Not yet can they manage big 'European-type' estate farming. Not yet can farm labourers get good wages. A European presence tends to make town life more attractive and the problems of urbanisation worse. This is especially true in the former French colonies where nearly all the expatriates are rich townsfolk, and in Kenya and Zambia where so many contract workers are.

The sort of expatriate a country needs is one who loves that country, its peoples and its customs; one who accepts its countrymen as equal even if less adept. He should at least speak their national language and perhaps a tribal one as well. But the sort who wants annual leave, Swiss bank accounts, perhaps dual nationality and such like.... presumably his heart lies abroad. (In like manner, those of Africa's politicians who own assets in Europe are somewhat suspect. Here the donkey gets no mitigation, for political leaders should be unselfish workhorses. Indeed, any African president who has feathered his own nest cannot really be regarded as stable. There are few who haven't; Nyerere comes immediately to mind. Banda, Mobutu and Kenyatta however are rich men.)

With a small and frugal expatriate presence, then, a country has much more hope in the building up of its own identity — a nationalism which means something. Gradually, over the years, tribal customs will be able to blend with the twentieth and subsequent centuries to form a national culture. In some countries, a few old tribal ways, as with Nigerian chiefs and emirs, are being encouraged and enforced by law. Sometimes, as in Tanzania, such titles no longer exist, and in Zaire, pygmies are now called 'petits Zairois'. The line between traditionalism and tribalism is extremely difficult for an emergent nationalist to draw.

To a certain extent, because of their national costumes, some Nigerians are immediately recognisable as such; a few, wearing pin-stripes in Lagos' tropical sun, remain anonymous. In Ethiopia, a country least of all affected by permanent colonialists, a national identity is more concrete. Already, modern national characteristics are developing on top of older ones; houses in Malawi and Zaire, guitar bands everywhere, women's hairstyles and dresses in Zaire, men's clothes in Zambia and Tanzania, all show individuality.

Now a culture is born when people communicate. Tribal customs still exist though many were and are badly shaken by Christianity and materialism respectively. Happily, some remain and will continue to do so because in all countries, each generation is taught its own tribal tongue. Tribal customs are carried by their tribal language. For a national culture, one must have a national, and natural, language. Neither English nor French fits the bill. Swahili is a natural Bantu language, acceptable to most tribes in East and parts of Central Africa. Zaire has four national languages and, considering its size, there is little wrong in that. Belgium afterall has two and she is tiny. Nigeria, because of her recent civil war, must rely on English for some years yet.

All countries learn English or French. This is necessary, rather like Latin was in Europe, while their own languages develop. No hurry. But towards a national identity, an 'authenticité' — even without a national language though such bastardisation is difficult to put over — all strive. The former French colonies, tied as they appear to be to France and her culture, will find life difficult when they join these current trends wholeheartedly. Congo Brazzaville and C.A.R. are trying. Cameroun, being an amalgam of former French and English territories, has a much bigger problem. (The above views on national languages are a little extreme. Many Africans even would disagree — probably the richer ones. Arguments in favour of the use of a European tongue are mainly educational-cum-economic, partly anti-tribal.)

In the schools of the former French colonies, little attempt, it would appear, is made towards African culture. French is sometimes taught throughout. Elsewhere, national or tribal languages are also taught though emphasis is given to the European one. Only in Tanzania is the national tongue given priority. There, Swahili is used as the language of instruction in all primary schools, while the minority who continue with a secondary education use English. The result is that everybody, nearly, is able to speak Swahili. Countrywide, regardless of tribe, the rich are able to talk to the poor. Peace will never be achieved anywhere without this. Other countries which have, in education, given simple economic considerations more weight, cannot so readily boast of national stability.

It is in the schools that the future lies. But the future, because it will be more educated, will need political leaders with higher principles and lower bank accounts, a freer press, a meaningful democracy and not a 'one-man-band', a nation of nationalists and internationalists but not of selfish and corrupt officials. Corruption is bad, especially in the richer nations. Compared with America's or India's, it is mild and unsubtle. But it exists and, on a small scale, it is widespread, even or especially in police forces. Corruption on top of capitalism on top of tribalism makes a potent stew. The young, as ever, are idealistic. Those who do not in their turn become caught in the system may wish to change it. But how, in a one-party system, do they do that?

A one-party democracy is certainly possible, but at present, in Central Africa, such a phenomenum is rare. In Gabon, one cannot ask questions. In Zaire, one can't criticise. In Kenya, elections are somewhat suspect. In Zambia candidates are vetted and in Uganda there is complete suppression. Often, MP's are yes-men while a president's rule is paramount. Banda has by decree, for instance, banned birth control and new maths (undemocratic but perhaps not unwise). Other rulers act in similar vein. But not one of the above wrongs or even a Burundi massacre makes another wrong, apartheid, right. (And meanwhile in Britain, bombs explode, people protest and MP's talk of their other interests. Who are we to criticise?)

The African is patient. As one Malawian put it, "Banda must die; then we'll have another go." But he is not very compassionate. Some Africans, a few soldiers, some policemen in Tanzania, 'les militants' in Zaire, the President in C.A.R., have got too much power too soon. The fellow African who criticises the system sometimes suffers, sometimes dies, sometimes 'floats down the Nile'. But the average African, especially if young and educated,

138

can see through the persistent wool of censored press releases, slogans, perpetual praises of the president, and so on. Eventually, Africa's politics will improve. It is inevitable, for they know what is wrong.

To The Future.

Two often heard cries are those of 'African socialism' and 'back to the land'. Meanwhile, the more materialistic school leaver is dreaming of that nice office job and the city life. Something is wrong. Even after academic failures, he feels work on the land is below him and undignified. Something is definitely wrong.

Central Africa needs agriculture. (And the word 'development' implies, does it not, that a foundation is already in existence — the agricultural, African, traditional way of life.) In years to come, Africa may hold the food weapon. In the meantime, she should start working. One must progress, slowly but surely. Those who are on the land should be encouraged to stay. Urbanisation is a plague, and unless it is checked, further food imports will be necessary. Compulsory repatriation of city slum dwellers does not and will never solve the problem. What one must do, surely, is change the system. Develop the rural areas, not the towns. Give the villages piped water, medical facilities, schools and, later perhaps, electricity. Make such food stuffs as they haven't got — milk, bread, beer — available at city prices, not city plus transport prices; Zambia is trying. Offer, like Cameroun does, good prices for farm produce. Arrange for its collection or process it in situ. When there is too much, export some. And so on. In a word, in order to develop, give the farm hand dignity and remove that air-conditioned white collar.

Surely here, in agriculture, is where aid can help. The rich world can help the development of labour intensive (economies of scale, those false gods, can be contemplated later) agricultural projects rather than city industries or prestigious white elephants. Aid can dig the well, construct the dam, clear the ground or build the in situ processing plant. Then, leaving few if any expatriates, it can retire and wait to buy what they want to sell: cow or eland, wheat or maize. If the Common Market food mountains are still high, this bought produce could be given to those who cannot help themselves — the drought victims of the sahel belt. In one move, one could aid two parts of the world. Or, via goatburgers or somesuch, one could increase the supply and lower the price of food in Britain — but that's another problem. And don't worry if, while Britons instruct in dairy farming, the Chinese build rice paddies. Afterall, Chinese expatriates, who are quite widespread in various agricultural projects, are not materialistically provocative. How much British aid or investment, one wonders, is spent on maintaining British expatriates at differentials formed in colonial times.

Parts of Central Africa are poor, but it is not the poverty of the 'have-nots' as in the slums of Calcutta. Rather, it is the poverty of the 'haves, but don't know what to do with'. Africa has the land. It needs, sometimes water, sometimes people, invariably more work. (What it also needs are 'grass-houses' — shades made from sticks and grass to protect young

139

seedlings from the scorching sun. A few, in Cameroun and Nigeria, are obviously most successful.) But it does not need Japanese tinned fish in Zaire, French sugar in Cameroun or Dutch textiles which are everywhere. For the time being, products like Dutch tinned milk are good for dietry reasons though the Kenyan products are probably equally nutritious. Food imports tend to discourage local development. Some parts of Africa are rich and, as they admit, if chaps didn't sit around drinking home made beer, they would be richer.

(Money alone as aid is not enough. As I have tried to point out, expatriates too are not the answer. Often they encourage urbanisation and slow down Africanisation, culturally if not industrially. And they make mistakes. One can understand why Zaire nationalised its petrol industries for competing garages around the same roundabout in Kinshasa do not constitute development. It is difficult to see how Zambia's best interests can be served in some of her mines, due for exhaustion in a decade or two, by short term contract workers. Some Europeans think next to nothing of the African and readily admit that they are abroad just for the money — it is the system, neo-colonial perhaps, that is at fault. Some are incompetent but, if they returned to Britain, they would probably be unemployed; in Africa, not only do they have a reasonable job but also subordinates if not servants. Others, many others, are doing a good job, for themselves perhaps but for their hosts as well. Expatriates are a good asset in the fight against tribalism.)

To return to the needs. Where Africa desperately needs water, there, there is poverty — the sahel belt. Donations of grain often fail to arrive — that 'ugly face' of corruption again. Local food, which could help drought stricken northern Nigeria, is sent south, for cities like Lagos offer higher prices. The compassion of one African for his fellow is minimal, but perhaps a few generations living above subsistence will change that. How to solve this drought problem in the short term?.... I don't know. But in the long term, is not the answer to provide water? Oil pipelines can stretch over thousands of miles; why not those of water? Perhaps, using Nigerian or Gabonese oil, sea water could be distilled and pumped to the river sources of, say, the Benue and the Logone in Cameroun. Thus Lake Chad could be kept topped up, and other areas too could have permanent water — the grain and cattle of country folk could survive. Corruption on this sort of aid, should, theoretically, be nil. This, I suggest, is one small but permanent part of the solution to the problem. But we must be quick. The drought, as rumoured, is spreading south. Some rivers in Zaire are at their lowest in living memory. Often, possibly through habit, people are burning precious vegetation, in Zaire, northern Nigeria, Cameroun and elsewhere. Only in Zambia and Malawi are instructions against such practice widespread. Here is another chance for aid — nature conservation — given the host country's consent. It would be more constructive than, say, the selling of automatic saws so popular in Cameroun. Some is already underway: for instance, afforestation in northern Nigeria.

Aid can and does help African agriculture. Africans too are playing their part, especially in those countries relying primarily on same, like Malawi and Tanzania. They, with Nigeria, Kenya and Cameroun seem to have agricultural

140

industries on their feet though in varying stages of growth. 'Come back to the land' policies tend to work better than 'go back to the land' ones. In Tanzania's ujamaa system, people are staying on the land and rural development is underway, albeit slowly. At least there, 'African socialism' means something. Few are the rich men, big houses and private cars, though personal incentives and private ownership still exist. Zaire's collectivités are further attempts but not so successful — the disparities between the copper workers/city dwellers and the country folk are too great, but so too are the distances.

To the future, then, what hope is there? Much. Give it time. In the long term, after at least decades, the fertile African countries should be self-sufficient agriculturally, industrially, totally, and they should be helping other less fortunate African states. There is this great potential. There are also many dangers. If Kenyatta does not hand over political power while he is still alive, there could be a nasty struggle. Later on, Banda will have the same problem. Gowon* faces a monumental task when he returns power to the politicians. Other generals, Amin, Mobutu, Bokassa, have no such intentions yet ... yet.

Where there is real hope is in Tanzania. There, tribal stress is small and such differences are not antagonised too greatly by those of wealth. One can but hope that ujamaa will bring agricultural self-sufficiency before aid runs out. She, by laying emphasis on slow development for all rather than fast for few, on agricultural development first and industrial second, is less worried by such factors as western inflation, oil crises and world recesses. Alas and of course, she too sufferes from corruption, white elephants and incomplete democracy. Zambia is trying to follow suit but has got off to a bad, cupric and capitalist start.

Individually and internationally, Africans wish for and are earning respect. Each nation, to varying extents, is striving for an identity. At the same time, none wish to throw away history, and friendship with the former colonialists is cherished. But each wants and needs complete independence: that is financial independence from stringy aid and their former European masters. More inter-Africa trade is possible and necessary. The former French colonies, where independence is as yet a little meaningless, are all somewhat tied together with common currencies and industries. It is at present too early for federations as the East African Community has shown.

The quest for respect is hampered by some political leaders who by their incompetence encourage supporters of apartheid. Others don't help much by speaking of embargoes with one hand while importing Rhodesian goods with the other. The Organisation of African Unity has definitely done some good. What it must now try to control are the likes of Amin, which is probably impossible, and oil or power struggles, which might be difficult. These could happen near Cabinda or near the Kenya/Ethiopia/Somalia border. Such acts

---

* The Nigerian coup of July 1975 replaced Gowon by Brigadier Murtali Mohammed**

** This book is out of date. Brigadier Mohammed has now been replaced by Lieutenant General Olusgun Obasanjo.

141

as the supplying of Russian arms to Somalia and Uganda are hardly likely to help peace. But, as outlined above, the West, which should be encouraging national and thereby international peace rather than just perpetuating western methods and culture with complete disregard for its inappropriateness, has not yet got clean hands.

P. J. E.
Belfast,
February, 1975.

POSTSCRIPT.

Often, travellers talk about luck, good fortune, chance and providence. Indeed, my story teller in this book has used such phrases.

I spent a lot of time by myself. While my legs were doing all the work, my head would often think. I felt small. In the jungle of Zaire, or in that canoe in the Atlantic, I felt less than small - a finite ant in an infinity of universe and time.

So many things could have gone wrong. Really successful adventurers always go through trials and perhaps sufferings. I have no right to compare myself with such men, if only because I have not sufficiently suffered. Any praise I receive, though, I cannot just by myself accept. No man, on such a journey, can look after himself by himself. Thankful for my safe return, I prefer to believe that a part, by no means insonsiderable, was played by a God.

I must also be thankful for the opportunity for such a journey. At a similar age, my father had had to fight a war. (And, during a spot of leave, me to conceive.)

KEY

1 shamba, mashamba — small African homestead(s), traditionally built, based on self-sufficient agriculture.

2 jambo — hallo.

3 mtoto, watoto — child, children.

4 dukah, madukah — small, open and not quite hygenic kiosk(s) selling simple produce. Some, those built in more recent years, are more sophisticated.

5 chai — tea.

6 ugali — or mealie meal. The food produced from maize; the staple carbohydrate of many parts of southern and eastern Africa.

7 shauri, mashauri — slang for noisy discussion(s) or argument(s); in correct Swahili, it means advice or plan(s).

8 native beer. — native beer.

9 baraza, mabaraza — meeting(s), usually conducted by an elder or even a government official.

10 mzungu, wazungu — European(s).

11 nini — what or thing-a-me-bob.

12 andazi, maandazi — buns(s): flour balls cooked in hot fat.

13 askari — sentry or nightwatchman.

14 hamatan* — north-easterly wind which blows from the Sahara over Cameroun and Nigeria for part of the year. During its season, everything outside is hazy, everything inside dusty.

15 foo-foo*, gari* — Nigerian foods prepared from yams.

16 bantu — a group of tribes resident in most parts of Central Africa.

17 piroque* — dug-out canoe.

---

*words associated, not with Swahili, a language born on the East coast of Central Africa, but with the more western countries.

144

CHRONOLOGY.

Some distances are, of course, approximations.

Date he left	from	No. of days cycling/ canoeing	Total Distance m	Total Distance km	Of which he cycled/ canoed m	Of which he cycled/ canoed km	His modes of transport	Date he arrived	At
17 Nov	Nairobi	9	585	941	560	901	bike, 1 lift	6 Dec	Mwanza
6 Dec	Mwanza	-	115	185	-	-	lake boat	7 Dec	Bukoba
7 Dec	Bukoba	4	201	324	195	315	bike, 2 lifts	10 Dec	Kisoro
10 Dec	Kisoro	-	614	988	-	-	police escort	15 Dec	Kisoro
15 Dec	Kisoro	11	637	1025	497	800	police escort to border, bike, 1 lift		
							riverboat	26 Dec	Kisangani
4 Jan	Kisangani	-	965	1554	143	230	bike, 1 lift	10 Jan	Kinshasa
12 Jan	Kinshasa	2	371	602	31*	50*	canoe and gunboat	13 Jan	Banana
15 Jan	Banana	2*	37*	60*	-	330	police escort, bike, lifts	16 Jan	Cabinda
21 Jan	Cabinda	8	1110	1788	205	1597	bike, 1 ferry	30 Jan	Yaounde
30 Jan	Yaounde	16	1000	1610	992	1127	bike	15 Feb	Lagos
24 Feb	Lagos	10	700	1127	700	-	rail	5 Mar	Kano
10 Mar	Kano	-	111	179	-	766	bike, 2 lifts	11 Mar	Zaria
11 Mar	Zaria	7	488	785	476	1483	bike, 1 lift	17 Mar	Yakoko
22 Mar	Yakoko	17	981	1580	921	208	canoe and riverboats	8 Apr	Bangui
9 Apr	Bangui	10*	800	1288	129	380	bike, lifts	2 May	Kinshasa
5 May	Kinshasa	5	674	1085	236	-	rail	10 May	Ilebo
12 May	Ilebo	-	1006	1619	-	1156	bike	15 May	Lubumbashi
15 May	Lubumbashi	10	718	1156	718	-	rail	25 May	Livingstone
27 May	Livingstone	-	295	475	-	3405	bike	28 May	Lusaka
1 Jun	Lusaka	31	2115	3405	2115			5 Jul	Nairobi
231		142	13523	21776	7918	12748			

* refers to passages in dug-out canoes. Maritime distances are tame guesses.

145

PERFORMANCE

Number of days spent:

canoeing	12
travelling by riverboat	18
under arrest	10
in trains	5
cycling	130

Average distance travelled per day under own steam:

counting every day	33m or 53km
counting only those days spent cycling/canoeing	59m or 95km

Least distance achieved in a full day's cycling:

(Zaire jungle – see page 26)   20m or 32km

Greatest distance achieved in a full day's cycling:

(last leg to Livingstone – see page 116)   117m or 187km

Total approximate cost:

in terms cash	£400
in terms pretty and educated brides	5

number of times washed sleeping bag   4

Total fuel consumption (lubricating oil)   ½ pint

Total number of

wheels used	5
tyres worn through	12
tubes exhausted	20
pairs of shoes worn out	8
punctures repaired	lost count

Number of times front wheel rotated:

(if all estimates are true)   6,139,341 and a bit

SPECIFICATIONS.

		Bike.	Baha.
1.	Type	Cheap	Usual
2.	Maker	Raleigh	Mum and Dad
3.	Version	Sports Gazelle	Mark 2
4.	Owner	One careless	Subject to nationalisation
5.	Frame	Hollow	Later please
6.	Gears	Nil - fixed ratio	One change of shorts
7.	Starting	First time	Sluggish
8.	Seat	One	Another, to match
9.	Suspension	Nil	One foam cushion fitted, after many boils on his bottom, in Nigeria
10.	Tyres	26 X 1¼ - 1⅝	Easily

Further copies of this book are obtainable from **P. J. Emerson** at **36 Ballysillan Road, Belfast 14.**

Also by the same author — "C by me", a philosophy by a molecule, available at the same address. Price 50p includes postage and packing.